The Best Dang Job in the World

A Leadership Guide for College and University Administrators

Bill Rezak

Hamilton Books

A member of
The Rowman & Littlefield Publishing Group
Lanham • Boulder • New York • Toronto • Plymouth, UK

Copyright © 2013 by Hamilton Books
4501 Forbes Boulevard, Suite 200, Lanham, Maryland 20706
Hamilton Books Aquisitions Department (301) 459-3366

10 Thornbury Road, Plymouth PL6 7PP, United Kingdom

All rights reserved

British Library Cataloguing in Publication Information Available

Library of Congress Control Number: 2013943664
ISBN: 978-0-7618-6193-5

For P
without whom I never would have been a college president
nor survived it.

Contents

Preface	vii
1 Sweet Failure — Such a Fine Teacher!	1
2 The First Interview	9
3 The Final Four — A Different Kind of March Madness!	13
4 The Offer	17
5 The Honeymoon Year	21
6 The Honey Fades from the Moon	39
7 Plans Begin to Coalesce	47
8 Friendraising and Fundraising	51
9 Reorganizing to Accommodate Fiscal Reality	63
10 You Have to Love It When the Plan Comes Together	69
11 Rules of the Road	75
12 The Centennial Celebration	81
13 Retirement	87
Appendixes	89

Preface

I have enjoyed three very different professional experiences. As an engineer, I was involved in the design and construction of coal-fired and nuclear power plants for 18 years. In my next incarnation I enjoyed higher education for 22 years, mostly as an administrator — the last 10 years were as a college president. And now I am a published author.

This book is a leadership guide for college and university administrators, especially presidents. It is based on my experiences and actions that I took. It derives from true events or composites thereof. The names of any real characters have been changed. I created a fictional college campus in a state where I did not serve as president.

This book is designed to be a light-hearted portrayal of a college presidency with "lessons learned." Implementation techniques are set forth for successful leadership of an academic enterprise and which are applicable "where the rubber meets the road." These include identifying, interviewing and hiring qualified college executives; decision-making; meeting management; time management; budget preparation and management; job descriptions and performance evaluations; strategic and operational planning and implementation; productivity assessment; and relationship building and fundraising.

This is a thorough guide for anyone aspiring to be a leader in higher education. It also focuses on personal characteristics and behaviors that point to success as a leader. I believe you will find this a fun, quick and worthwhile read.

Chapter One

Sweet Failure — Such a Fine Teacher!

"Would you like me to give you a formula for success? It's quite simple, really. Double your rate of failure. You are thinking of failure as the enemy of success, but it isn't at all. You can be discouraged by failure or you can learn from it, so go ahead and make mistakes. Make all you can, because remember that's where you will find success." —Thomas J. Watson

Rick Nedic's (pronounced Ned'-ich) father was a Croat immigrant and his mother was an American of Anglo-Saxon descent. He met his bride, Sally Cochrane, at Farmington State University in New Mexico in 1975. He was finishing up his doctoral studies in behavioral psychology while teaching undergraduate students part time. Sally was a student in one of his classes.

Rick was tall and lean — about 6'-3" and 180 lbs. Sally, at 5'-2", was much shorter and very cute. They dated after she had completed the course. One thing led to another and they lived together for a while before marrying.

College and university presidents represent and, if artful, can effectively utilize a relatively large pool of exceptionally talented people. All this talent can accomplish grand things, if effectively mobilized. Presidents also have a bully pulpit from which to expound upon the issues of the day, be they related to higher education or to society in general.

Rick was offered the presidency of Black Rock State College (BRSC) in rural Clayton, Georgia in the early spring of 2001. Up until that time, he had generated a reasonably impressive record of achievement in academic circles marching through the various levels of professorial rank to that of tenured full professor at Wellsboro State College in Wellsboro, Pennsylvania ten years after earning his doctorate. Sally and he married shortly after moving to Wellsboro.

Rick accepted a position as chair of the psychology department at Grable State College in Slidell, Louisiana a few years later at age 39. At age 44, he applied for and was appointed Dean of the College of Arts & Sciences at Middle Arkansas State University in Mt. Nuenemacher, Arkansas where he served successfully for eight years.

As is true for most college and university leaders, Rick had good interpersonal skills, a quick mind, a learned skill of remembering peoples' names, an excellent feel for the financial side of public higher education, a high energy level, and he was charismatic. He had also garnered skill at strategic planning and was an effective relationship builder and fundraiser.

One of Rick's challenges was managing his strong need for achievement. This frequently led to impatience with the methodical and excruciatingly slow pace of progress in the academy. His impression was that colleges and universities loved to study issues ad nauseam with little sense of urgency. It seemed to him that faculty deliberations were prone to focus on the trivial. He had heard this called being caught up "in the thick of thin things" which he thought was particularly après pro. It reminded him of the play on words from Sir Winston Churchill's famous 1940 World War II speech, "Never was so little owed by so few to so many."

This impatience extended to those faculty who Rick dubbed "briefcase professors." These folks were on campus long enough to conduct their classes, kept few office hours for students, and then ran off to lucrative consulting opportunities made possible by the credibility that the university bestowed upon them as subject matter experts and their teaching schedules which allowed ample time for such undertakings. His preference was that they work their consulting assignments through the College of Arts & Sciences so that it could generate overhead revenue and exposure from this activity.

Middle Arkansas State University (MASU) was a medium sized regional university with no strategic plan. The president perhaps believed that the environment was changing so rapidly as to make planning a useless endeavor. Maybe she thought that as soon as well thought out plans were developed, circumstances changed and rendered them either obsolete or unattainable.

The faculty *loved* this approach! They were happy teaching their classes and then conducting research, writing, or consulting as they saw fit with no concern for the future well-being of the institution as a whole.

This drove Rick nuts! He wanted to be able to utilize faculty resources in moving the College of Arts & Sciences and the University toward some over-arching goals and objectives. No single university official or group of officials could hope to make progress toward institutional objectives without buy-in and active participation of the faculty and staff with their many and varied talents. So, Rick set about developing a strategic plan for the College of Arts & Sciences. The academic department chairs and faculty who reported to him resented having to spend time and energy at this endeavor when the rest of the university was not required to do so.

Over a period of several months and after he had been serving as dean for seven years, the College of Arts & Sciences department chairs and their faculties slowly and deliberately put together a revolt against Rick's constant press for innovation, improvement, strategic planning and consulting through university auspices. They interpreted this as heavy-handedness on his part. They also assumed that he was driven by ambition for himself, not for the university. Some of both were at work, Rick was certain. This ultimately resulted in a vote of no confidence in his leadership.

The Provost (to whom the deans reported) backed Rick. Rick expected that the President might also back an effective dean — you might suppose that he would think that he was effective — and that a no-confidence vote might result in the dean adjusting his approach to reduce pressure on faculty.

The MASU president was brilliant. A voracious reader, she kept up with the latest developments in her field of expertise and in higher education. She was well informed on the issues of the day in politics and business and industry, as well. She was thoughtful and articulate. Rick also believed that she tolerated some incompetent people in key administrative positions. He complained to Sally about this so often that she finally requested that he refrain from further commentary unless he was willing to leave!

One officer who *was* worth his salt was the Provost and Vice President for Academic Affairs, Rick's immediate boss. He was a superior counselor and tactician. The Provost surrounded himself with excellent people. Again, you might suppose that Rick would think so! He understood his own shortcomings — he was not good at implementation. Strategy and analysis were his strong suits, so he gathered around him a group comprised of excellent implementers. Good leaders understand themselves well enough to recognize their strengths and weaknesses, and to then hire people who complement the short-comings.

It seemed to Rick that the president was regularly confronted by obstreperous faculty who challenged many of her decisions. He believed that she had difficulty earning the trust of the campus at large. Rick attributed this to her unwillingness or inability to engage individual members of the organization in a personal, interested, and caring manner. The trust of others is earned one person at a time through constant, thoughtful, honest interaction with each. Weak or little interaction results in lack of understanding and trust. The position of authority in itself creates barriers to communication that it is incumbent upon the leader to overcome.

The president's considerable accomplishments were partially overshadowed by her inability to earn the trust and respect of her constituency. She was an excellent spokesperson for the university's needs and offerings. Rick thought that she may have been concerned about job security and did not wish to deal with internal trauma which might rock the boat or disrupt faculty. Rick quickly found himself a dean without a purview.

He was able to negotiate a relatively high-paying tenured faculty position at MASU. This prospect, however, did not particularly excite him. At age 52, he didn't see himself going back into the classroom on a full-time basis.

Rick was depressed about the chain of events. He was, however, with the help of Sally, able to develop a healthy perspective on the situation. Rather than blaming university leadership for his misfortune, Rick swallowed hard and conducted a diagnostic review of the things he had done that had resulted in this unsatisfactory outcome. He knew that he had pressed too hard for change in the College of Arts & Sciences. There is nothing quite like failure to focus the mind on the need for different approaches.

Successful leaders have the strength of character to accept responsibility for the outcomes they produce. Some of today's corporate, military, political, and other leaders seem to try to avoid taking responsibility for the outcomes that they and their organizations realize. This would shock the likes of Abraham Lincoln, Winston Churchill, Harry Truman, George Patton, Dwight Eisenhower, Jack Kennedy, Martin Luther King, Jr., Vince Lombardi, Jimmy Carter, and Ted Turner. They recognize(d) that, as leaders, they bore/bear ultimate responsibility for everything their administrations or organizations did/do.

Owning the results we produce is a terrific learning experience. There is no better teacher than dealing with the consequences of our actions. Blaming others for undesirable outcomes limits growth. The leaders listed above experienced significant failures and setbacks in their professional lives. They learned valuable lessons from these unpleasant outcomes and recovered to achieve great things.

It's easy to bask in the glow of positive outcomes and successes. Not so for failures. Some leaders tend to rationalize ways to avoid the embarrassment of owning negative results. They try to convince themselves, and perhaps others, that someone else's shortcomings are to blame. That is seldom the case.

Rick was a longtime observer of the hundreds of people in whose professional lives he had been responsible for providing leadership, and the several who led the organizations of which he was a member. It amazed him how some people sought out significant organizational responsibility for the associated recognition, prestige and salary; and, then tried to avoid the results of their performance and that of the team they led.

One of the keys to surviving a setback while others gloat is to "never let the sons-of-bitches see you sweat!" Always remain calm and outwardly unperturbed, no matter how outrageous the claims. Be gracious when others are being obnoxious. Your professionalism will unnerve the abuser; and your magnanimity will impress your constituents.

Keeping cool under fire is an invaluable asset. A team will be more apt to follow a leader when the leader is viewed as having the strength to remain stable, unperturbed, and solid under stress.

You may be familiar with this story of failure and success. It's about a young man who suffered a business failure at age 31. He was defeated in a state legislative election at age 32. Two years later, he failed in business again. The woman he loved died when he was 35, leading him to a nervous breakdown the following year. He lost another state legislative election at age 38, and a US Congressional race when 43. When he was 47, he lost still another Congressional race. He achieved the same result at age 49. At age 55, he lost election to the US Senate. He failed in a quest to become Vice President of the United States at age 56. He lost another US Senate election at 58. At age 60, this remarkable man became President of the United States of America. His name was Abraham Lincoln.

Lincoln was one of the most reflective leaders history has recorded. He constantly evaluated the results he produced. He never shirked responsibility and he was enormously effective.

President Bill Clinton states the following in his informative book, *My Life,* as he discusses losing a gubernatorial election in Arkansas. "…if I hadn't been defeated, I probably never would have become president. It was a near-death experience; but, an invaluable one, forcing me to become more sensitive to political problems in progressive politics: the system can absorb only so much change at once; no one can beat all the entrenched interests at the same time; and, if people think you've stopped listening, you're sunk."

Rick's greatest failures resulted in dramatic learning and growth. His deanship had many accomplishments of which he was proud. Enrollment grew expansively, new academic programs were initiated including the College's first doctoral degree, and external funding increased sharply. The College received a seven figure grant from a major US corporation. All this occurred with his constant press for improvement.

In the end, however, Rick's deanship failed. He spent a good deal of time analyzing what went wrong. At best, he could say that he got too far out in front of the College with his many initiatives. In reality, the faculty he presumed to lead simply decided they didn't want him to be their leader any longer.

This was the single best learning experience of Rick's professional life. For a brief period, his confidence took a nose dive. He groped for insight into what he would do next. He was a tenured faculty member and could return to the classroom, if he so chose. As previously mentioned, however, Rick suffered from a pressing need for achievement. He decided that he could not stop striving for something more special, so he began to look for other opportunities.

One of the faculty in the College of Arts and Sciences tried to convince Rick that he should accept his fate and remain a faculty member in the College he had led. This person suggested that he thought that Rick was being disloyal to consider leaving. That, to Rick, was surrendering control of his professional destiny to others. Time to fire MASU and hire another college or university!

Changing organizations after a major failure or with some regularity is a good move. It is difficult for the leaders and the members of the old organization to overcome the idea that you have tripped up and are, therefore, damaged goods. Changing organizations allows us to reinvent ourselves. No one in the new organization knows much about a new leader. A fresh start is uplifting. People in the old organization are skeptical that you can change. People in the new organization *expect* that a new leader will be changing things. They don't know that the leader is undergoing great change, as well. This is an amazingly positive and refreshing dynamic!

Rick thought that leaders should change organizations every eight to 12 years, regardless of the circumstances. Leaders create baggage in their working lives. This baggage sticks like glue. People who knew an aspiring leader as a young person in an organization may always view that person as "wet behind the ears," inexperienced and not yet ready for more responsibility. When you change organizations, people assume that you are capable of doing whatever you were hired to do.

Embracing failure is not easy, especially the first time. No one, however, who has tried to do anything the least bit difficult, has avoided it. The key is not to be debilitated by failure, but to learn from it and to change the approach to the next opportunity.

Sally and Rick spent a good deal of time assessing the situation. She was his most valued advisor and ardent supporter. She had long urged him to leave MASU due to his poor opinion of the university's leadership. They decided that now, with their children grown and out of the house, might be an opportune time to think about a move.

Rick sought the advice of some of his non-MASU professional colleagues. These were members of the Mt. Neunemacher business community and colleagues from other colleges and universities. They were supportive and several offered to provide positive references for him. One offered to nominate him for college presidencies.

When Rick was approached in the fall of 2000 by an executive recruiting firm (which had been contacted by his nominator) regarding the presidency of Black Rock State, he wondered if he had the will, desire, ability and tenacity to be a college president. He saw the sacrifices that the president of MASU made every day. A college presidency amounted to life in a fish bowl with unending commitments to attend the functions and activities of every group and organization on campus. The president's day frequently began with a 7:00 AM breakfast meeting and ended with a student theatrical production, choir performance, or athletic or social club event which might last until 10:00 PM. Was that an appealing prospect? How would Sally adjust to all that?

They turned the invitation over in their minds and decided that it would be a fun learning experience to apply for the job, the odds being long of actually receiving an offer of employment from a pool of from 50 to 75 applicants. Rick researched Black Rock State in order to learn a bit about it. He reviewed the college's web site and its academic offerings. Then he sent along a brief two page resume (he abhorred curriculum vitae a quarter inch thick full of trivia that no one reads!) accompanied by a one page cover letter pointing out some of the characteristics of Black Rock State that he thought best fit his qualifications. It was October of 2000 and Sally and he turned their attention to other things.

At the end of fall semester, they and their two adult children (unmarried at the time) gathered at their Ozark Mountain vacation cottage for the holiday season. After a quiet New Year's Day of food and football they returned to their respective homes.

Had Rick still been Dean of Arts & Sciences, he would have begun to prepare for an academic retreat to plan projects for the spring semester. He would have dissected the College of Arts & Sciences' strategic plan and assigned various parts of it to each of the department heads who reported to him. He would have required that they, in turn, assign pieces of the plan to the faculty and staff members who reported to each of them. In this way, the strategic goals were divided into bite-sized action item chunks with all organizational members involved in their attainment.

Faculty in the College of Arts & Sciences were evaluated annually based partially upon their ability to successfully address these assigned strategic tasks, as well as on their teaching performance. This was another reason that Rick's popularity as dean was on the wan! The faculty of the other colleges at MASU had no such responsibilities or evaluations.

This semester, however, Rick found himself on special assignment with no meaningful responsibilities. He, therefore, filled his time searching for interesting looking professional opportunities.

One of several messages left on their home phone when they returned from their holiday was from the executive search firm handling the presidential search for Black Rock State College. The message asked that Rick call as soon as possible. He knew that they would not be calling if they were not interested in his candidacy.

"Here we go, Sally!" he exclaimed.

"Well, you've got to call them back, Sweetie." Sally smiled.

"I know, I know! And I hope you understand where this might lead." Rick suggested with excitement.

"We'll just take it one step at a time." his lifelong partner replied with a grin.

Rick got pen and paper and reviewed some of his notes taken from the BRSC website. Then, assuming that he might be invited for an interview, he made a list of material he thought he'd like to review prior to such an occasion. With this preparation, he called the head-hunter whose name was Nancy Block.

"Ms. Block, this is Rick Nedic returning your call regarding the Black Rock State College search." He identified myself.

"Please call me Nancy." she answered with a smile in her voice. "I'm hoping that we're going to be spending a good deal of time together. Black Rock State would like to visit with you in person about their presidency. They would like you to come to campus for an interview at their expense and I have several dates for you to consider, all of which are about a month off."

"Well that's very nice Nancy. I'm delighted and please call me Rick. How many are being invited?

"They're going to invite eight or 10 initially. They will then cut to three or four finalists and conduct a second interview." said Nancy. "Spouses will be included on the second trip."

This, Rick knew, was standard operating procedure for college and university presidential searches. He asked Nancy if it would be appropriate to request some additional information about the college. She encouraged him to request whatever he might like directly from the BRSC president's office, as the Executive Assistant to the President had been tasked with providing such information to prospective candidates.

She asked Rick some questions about his qualifications and reasons for believing that he might be a good fit for BRCS. She also asked for a list of references. She then explained that the college's presidential search committee was comprised of a selection of President's Advisory Council members, vice presidents and deans and a few faculty and staff members along with a representative of the Chancellor of the University System of Georgia, to whom the BRSC president reported and a student, would be involved in the first interview. She then scheduled a mutually acceptable date for him to come to campus.

After he hung up the phone, Rick looked long and hard at Sally.

"I can see myself getting caught up in this!" he laughed.

"Like I said, Big Boy, one step at a time, please." responded the person whose opinions he valued more than any other.

Chapter Two

The First Interview

> *"Successful and unsuccessful people do not vary greatly in their abilities. They vary in their desires to reach their potential."* —John Maxwell

Rick set about refining the list of information he wanted to request in order to prepare for the interview. It included the Black Rock State strategic plan (if there was one), an annual budget summary with five years of history, an organization chart, a faculty/staff directory (preferably with pictures), enrollment and graduation statistics by academic program for the past several years, the latest annual report, endowment details including investment strategy, the names of members of the President's Advisory Council (a group of influential local citizens appointed by the governor as a resource for the president) and the names and affiliations of members of the Presidential Search Committee.

He also wanted to familiarize himself with the academic programs at the College and the names of the faculty involved with each. Some of this information was available on the college's website. He studied the names of the key administrators and department leaders.

After the requested material arrived, Rick digested the budget, organization chart, enrollment and graduation stats, size of the endowment and major accomplishments of the last year. He then set about anticipating questions he thought might be posed in the upcoming interview. A list of these appears in Appendix I.

Rick thought out responses to these questions, along with an explanation of his current "dean without a purview" situation at MASU and rehearsed them with Sally, a psychology major herself. She helped him fine-tune his message and he rehearsed some more. He began to feel confident about his insight regarding Black Rock State College, its programs, its financial situation and its plans and challenges for the future. He was ready to put his best foot forward.

Rick's interview was scheduled for Tuesday, February 3, 2001. He didn't know where he was in the sequence of candidates. He would have preferred to be toward the end of the multiple interviews. He believed that the decision-makers were more apt to remember best those who had been interviewed most recently. Rick decided that he would make an issue of that during the second round of interviews, should he make it that far.

He flew into Atlanta early on the day before the interview and drove a rental car the 100 plus miles northeast to Clayton, Georgia. That gave him some daylight hours to look around and assess the amenities. Rick had a reservation at the Old Clayton Inn, a venerable rustic hotel in the heart of the small town of a little over 2000 people. On Main St., he wondered about the significance of The Rock House and made a mental note of the Clayton Café, the Bear Creek Café and Rumor Hazit Restaurant. Prater's Main Street Book Store looked interesting and he stopped at Mountain Nature & Wild Bird Supply to purchase a bird feeder to take home to Sally.

He was glad to discover the Clayton Tribune newspaper. It was a pleasant community and Rick decided that, while "centrally isolated," it was in beautiful country and that Clayton had some reasonable shopping and dining options. Rick called Sally and gave her an account of his observations.

"Break a leg!" she encouraged him.

The next morning, Reggie Bloyston, Director of Counseling Services at the college and a member of the search committee, picked him up at the Old Clayton Inn. They had an amicable drive to the close-by college. Prior to meeting with the committee, Dr. Bloyston drove him through the campus. It was about 60 acres in size with an enrollment of approximately 4000 students. The buildings were gathered around a center quadrangle in a typical college cluster. The architecture was squarish post World War II brick — clean and neat, if not exceptional. The residence halls accommodated about 3000 students. The remainder, all upper classmen, rented rooms or apartments in and around Clayton.

The Presidential Search Committee was comprised of three members of the President's Advisory Council, one of whom was the committee chair; the Provost, who was also Vice President of Academic Affairs; the academic Dean of Business Administration; the Director of Development, responsible for fundraising; a faculty member from each of the college's four schools of study; the president of the student body; the chair of the Faculty Senate; and the Executive Assistant to the President. Also participating was a representative of the Chancellor of the University System of Georgia, Nancy Block representing the executive search consultant and Dr. Bloyston.

Dr. Bloyston escorted Rick to the conference room where the search committee awaited. Rick had memorized the names of all the players, so now it was just a matter of connecting faces with names. He found that, after being introduced, if he utilized each person's name in conversation as soon as possible, he remembered who was who.

Rick was asked to make an opening statement. He was well prepared for this, having studied the college's existing plans and what he believed to be its challenges. He also decided to take this opportunity to address head-on his situation at Middle Arkansas State. Rick explained that he believed that he had been too aggressive in pressing for development of a strategic plan for the College of Arts & Sciences and in attempting to rein in "briefcase faculty." He acknowledged that he had learned a valuable lesson here and suggested that the search committee contact the Provost or President at MASU if they wished their perspectives on the situation.

He then launched into a conversation regarding his qualifications and the experiences that he believed were applicable to the initiatives already underway and those that would be required to confront the challenges that lay ahead for BRSC. Eye contact with the members of the committee assured him that these thoughts were resonating with the group.

After Rick's opening statement, the committee initiated a set of predetermined questions very much like those that he had anticipated. He was able to handle these with ease, thanks to the careful preparation and rehearsing he had done with Sally playing the role of interviewer and to his over 30 years as a student, faculty member and leader on college campuses.

Rick's assessment was that the interview with the search committee went well. From there he moved to an interview with the group of people who reported directly to the president. This encounter was much like the first and he felt good about it, as well.

He was then escorted by one of the academic department chairs on a walking tour of the campus. Rick found this to be interesting and informative. He was able to begin to form an opinion about academic life at BRSC.

Lunch was next with the academic deans. Since he was literally one of them, Rick was able to relate easily to their issues and challenges. This also presented an opportunity for him to provide some information about himself, as well as to gain some insight into the operation of the four separate schools of study at the college.

And then his visit was over. Rick had an opportunity to ask a few last minute questions of his host, Dr. Boylston on the way back to pick up the rental car. Then, he headed for Atlanta and a late flight home.

Chapter Three

The Final Four — A Different Kind of March Madness!

> *"The secret of success is to do the common things uncommonly well."*
> —John D. Rockefeller

Rick received a phone call a couple of weeks later from Nancy Block informing him that he had made the cut to a final group of four candidates who would be invited back for a second and more thorough round of interviews over a period of three days and including spouses. He shared the news with Sally, a big grin on his face.

"You're really enjoying this, aren't you?" she kidded.

"I now have a *huge* advantage over the other candidates!" Rick pronounced. "*I* have a secret weapon! I will have the *most* personable and impressive spouse of all! They're going to *love* you!"

Twenty five years of marriage had proven beyond a shadow of a doubt that he had married a special woman of substance. She was as at ease in her own skin as anyone Rick had ever known. There simply was not "an air" about her. She was grounded and forthright and literally never met a stranger. People who spent time with her felt that they must be the most important person in her life. She was that warm and empathetic.

"We'll see." Sally shrugged.

"Well, I'll tell you one thing. I learned a bit about the current president during my first visit and, if they want more of the same, we're out. But, if they're looking for the exact opposite, we have a shot!"

Rick knew that it was almost a certainty that groups searching for a new leader will seek one who is a polar opposite of the predecessor. The current president (who was retiring after seven years) was, in Rick's assessment, very bright, hard-working and effective with excellent insight into the higher education enterprise. Rick's inquiries convinced him that the campus saw the president as sober of personality and introverted. Sally and he waited for the call setting up their appointment for the second interview.

Eventually, Nancy Block called back and arranged dates for them to travel to Clayton together for two days of interviews on campus and a third day in Atlanta with the Chancellor of the University System of Georgia. Rick was advised that they would be the third of four finalists to be interviewed. He decided not to press his luck and accepted, grateful to be second to last.

Sally had worked in human resources in the business world for a few years after they began living together. She continued this until their children were born. Then, she chose to be a stay-at-home mother for several years while the children were small. When they moved to Louisiana, she went back into the business world as an organizational effectiveness consultant.

Rick always felt guilty that he kept disrupting her career to further his own; but Sally didn't seem to mind. She was proud of his drive and was more interested in her children than developing a career. She always seemed to see these disruptions as a new adventure.

They decided to drive to Georgia so as to have more time to look around without running up BRCS's costs too much. It was an enjoyable one day trek. They gave themselves a day in the area before the interview process commenced.

The Nedics found Clayton and surrounds beautiful. It sat in the foothills of the lovely Blue Ridge Mountains. Dams on the Tallulah River formed Lakes Burton, Seed and Rabun to the south. Lake Rabun emptied into Tallulah Gorge where the movie *Deliverance* was filmed and where in 1970, 65 year old Karl Wallenda tight rope walked across from one side of the precipice to the other.

To the north was beautiful Black Rock Mountain State Park and Warwoman Wildlife Management Preserve. Sally especially enjoyed the Warwoman moniker. There was plenty of outdoor activity available that was for certain.

On the first day of interviews, one of the President's Advisory Council members came to meet them for breakfast at the Old Clayton Inn. They had received in advance a copy of their itinerary for the visit. The first day called for them to split up. Sally, who had not been introduced to the region, would be escorted on a tour of Clayton and the surrounding area, a tour of the campus, and then to meetings with student activities staff members. Rick would meet with the entire President's Advisory Council, with the search committee again, and with students. Sally was scheduled for lunch with some of the Advisory Council; Rick with some of the search committee.

In the afternoon, both of them would meet together with faculty and staff in sessions designed to familiarize them with the issues most important to those groups. In these settings, campus personnel were able to glean a sense of how Sally and Rick might represent them to the public. This is where he knew that Sally would especially shine.

Rick took the thoughtful approach to responding to questions in these afternoon sessions. Sally, ever the cut-up, took herself much less seriously. He gave professionally credible responses; and then Sally would supplement his offerings with something witty designed to lighten the conversation and show their human side. They didn't rehearse this; indeed, they didn't even discuss it. It was simply the different way in which they viewed the world. It was also part of the chemistry that made their relationship healthy and fun and a growth experience for both.

Rick was asked how he would find time as president to deal with the issues of the day and still have an opportunity to be a visible presence on campus.

"Well," he began, "I don't like to spend my time during the day doing paper work in my office. I'd rather be out and about campus and do the paper work at home in the evening."

Sally didn't say a word. Sitting next to him at a table in front of the group, she simply pointed to him with a frustrated look on her face, rolled her eyes and nodded her head up and down. This brought down the house and established instant rapport. They were at ease with one another and in relating to their audience.

"Can't take her anywhere!" Rick cracked wise.

That evening, they were escorted to dinner by members of the Advisory Council and some of the search committee. Thus, many of the college's stakeholders were able to observe and interact with candidates in various kinds of forums. The experience was at the same time exhilarating and exhausting.

The next day was a repeat of the first with different groups of people from the campus — those in food service, residence hall management, athletics, the business office, admissions, physical plant, financial aid, registrar and students. By the end of the day, the Nedics couldn't remember what they had said to which group — it all ran together in their minds.

On the morning of the third day, they drove the approximately 110 miles to Atlanta for an interview with the Chancellor of the University System of Georgia. The Georgia system of public higher education consisted of over 30 colleges and universities with total enrollment in excess of 300,000 students. The flagship campuses of the System were the University of Georgia, Georgia Tech and Georgia State University. Black Rock State College was one of the smaller campuses. It did, however, serve a large geographic area of the northeastern portion of the state.

Chancellor Mike Talbot and Rick were the same age. He had already been a successful college president and had been appointed Chancellor for the System five years ago. All of the system presidents reported to Talbot who, in turn, reported to a Board of Regents appointed by the governor. Talbot and Rick spent an hour together and Rick came away feeling that the dialogue had gone well. He found Talbot to be open and forthright with a clear and supportive understanding of Black Rock State's role in the System.

On the following day, Sally and Rick drove back to Arkansas. The search committee chair had indicated that a selection decision would be made within two or three weeks. They went home and tried to immerse themselves in their daily lives — easier for Sally than Rick!

Chapter Four

The Offer

"It is not the critic who counts, nor the man who points out how the strong man stumbled or where the doer of deeds could have done them better. The credit goes to those who are actually in the arena, who strive valiantly; who know the great enthusiasms, the great devotions, and spend themselves in a worthy cause; who at the best, know the triumph of high achievement; and who, at the worst, if they fail, fail while daring greatly, so that their place shall never be with those cold and timid souls who know neither victory nor defeat."
—President Theodore Roosevelt

Sure enough, the chair of the search committee (who had been authorized by the Chancellor) called Rick on a Saturday morning in late March 2001. She excitedly indicated that he was the preferred candidate and that the Chancellor's representative would be calling with an explanation of the details and an official offer of employment with a letter of confirmation on its way. Rick reacted with excitement of his own and told the chair that he would call back with a response within a day or two of speaking with the Chancellor's Office.

Later that same day, the Chancellor's representative, who had been involved in the interview process, called to tender a formal offer contingent upon Board of Regents approval. The college had a campus home where the president was asked to reside. There was a new car included in the package, as well as health insurance and other fringe benefits. Also of importance, since the president served at the pleasure of the Chancellor, was a tenured faculty position at any one of the System campuses in the event that the presidency didn't work out. The salary was $145,000.

Rick hung up the phone and took a deep breath. Sally was excited as he explained the details of the offer.

"Well we have to accept!" she exclaimed with excitement.

"I think it's a terrific fit for me, Sweetie, but how are you going to enjoy life in rural Georgia? What will you find to do there?" Rick was concerned that she would go along just to be supportive.

"I'll bloom where I'm planted." she declared matter-of-factly. "It sounds like a grand adventure to me. When do we go?"

"They want me on board by July 1st."

"Good, that gives us time to prepare." she posited.

"Let's sleep on it over the weekend." He suggested. "I'll call them back on Monday with a decision."

And so they did. Rick was smitten with the job, the campus, the countryside and the anticipation. Sally was resolute that he needed this final challenge/opportunity to fulfill his professional aspirations. She was a bit frightened at the prospect, but imagined that she could find something meaningful to do with herself in Clayton separate from Rick and the college. She failed to realize how difficult this was to be for her.

Rick was afraid that Sally wasn't considering the impact of leaving behind her many friends in Arkansas, to say nothing of the house in which their children had been raised. Nonetheless, he was so elated at the prospect that he couldn't believe that it would be anything other than a terrific experience for both of them.

They talked of little else all weekend. On Monday, Rick called and accepted the offer. There was still one more hurdle. He had to be appointed by act of the University System of Georgia Board of Regents. That meant another trip to Atlanta to meet with the Regents and to be present at one of their monthly board meetings for their action regarding his appointment. This was scheduled to occur at their April 2001 meeting, a few weeks hence.

Rick struggled with how to break the news to the Middle Arkansas State community. He, of course, immediately informed the President and Provost, both of who had been supportive of his desire to become a college president (and to be shut of him, he was certain!) and who had served as references for him. The President of MASU suggested that they wait to make a formal announcement until after the Georgia Board of Regents had acted on Rick's appointment. That way, there would be no premature conclusions. Unfortunately, they were not allowed that luxury.

A BRSC faculty member, curious about this new guy, Nedic, had called a colleague at MASU to get the lowdown on Rick from a counterpart's perspective. Rick happened to be close to this particular MASU faculty member. To his credit, he immediately called Rick to advise of the call from BRSC.

How inappropriate, Rick thought, reflecting on the BRSC faculty member's call. Then he checked himself, realizing that he was now to be a public official living in a professional and personal fish bowl. Rick wondered if Sally realized the implications of this.

The MASU president at this point suggested issuing an announcement regarding Rick's impending move, subject to Georgia Board of Regents approval. This, she correctly believed, would put to rest speculation churning out of the campus rumor mill. And so it became public knowledge in early April 2001 that Rick would be leaving MASU.

Later that month he flew to Atlanta, this time to undergo an interview with several Regents, one of whom then nominated him for the position of president of Black Rock State College. And so it was done. Now Rick had two and one half months to hand off his responsibilities at Middle Arkansas State (little as they were!), study up on BRSC and move.

Sally and he decided that she would accompany him at the end of June only if their home and the building which housed her consulting business both sold before then. Neither did and so Sally remained behind for almost six months to tend to these details. They packed up the car to the brim with enough clothing and other necessities to sustain Rick on his own for this interim period until she sold the house and had their furniture moved.

Rick made a strategic decision regarding the designation of the president's house. He decided to call it the College Home in the hope that the campus community would begin to see it as a component of the overall physical plant.

The home was built in 1908 and was quite elegant. It had been acquired by the college in 1964. It underwent significant renovation and expansion in the late '70s. On the main floor was a large living room with lovely fire place (which was inoperable because the local fire marshal had deemed the chimney unsafe!), a formal dining room that would seat 12, a large modern eat-in kitchen with new appliances, and an enormous great room adequate for most receptions or which could seat another 30 for a meal. There was also a full bath on the main floor.

Upstairs was a large master bedroom and bath with two connecting offices, and three guest bedrooms with another full bath. The house had a large unfinished attic and basement, as well as a two car garage. It was situated in stately fashion atop a knoll overlooking the town of Clayton about two blocks from the BRSC campus — just far enough to garner some privacy the Nedics thought.

Sally, as was mentioned, remained behind in Arkansas to close up the house in which they had raised their family. She and Rick had long ago made plans to retire to their mountain retreat in the Ozarks, so Rick minimized the impact that selling the house where their family had generated so many fond memories would have on Sally. He was off on an exciting new adventure and she was left behind to deal with the remnants of their previous life. It was not a happy time for her and Rick failed to empathize with her experience.

They planned long weekend get-togethers alternating between Arkansas and Georgia about every three weeks. They spoke on the phone every evening, but somehow this wasn't satisfying. Rick was excited to bring Sally up to speed with the latest college developments and she wanted him to share in the emotional upheaval she was feeling. There was a serious issue of re-entry as each of them attempted to share issues of import from their different perspectives. It was a stressful time for both of them.

The Nedic's home in Arkansas finally sold in late fall. The office building that housed Sally's consulting business remained on the market, selling in early 2002. Sally was able to arrive in Clayton to meet the moving van with their furniture in December 2001. It was a happy reunion, although she never thought that Rick fully appreciated her trauma in walking away alone from their home in Arkansas.

Speaking of the children, they joined Sally and Rick for the holidays in their new home. It was a wonderful family reunion.

Chapter Five

The Honeymoon Year

> *"Desire is the key to motivation, but it's the determination and commitment to an unrelenting pursuit of your goal — a commitment to excellence — that will enable you to attain the success you seek."* —Mario Andretti

Rick thought long and hard about how to roll out his administration and its new agenda to the BRSC campus. He had an opportunity to recreate himself in this new setting, since no one knew anything about him. There was something very refreshing about being able to start over with a clean slate and no baggage.

As frequently happens when a new administration arrives, some of the leaders of the previous one chose to retire or move on. The Vice Presidents of Administration (finance and budget, human resources, physical plant, food service and information technology) and of Student Affairs (student activities, athletics, residential life, enrollment management, admissions and financial aid) retired as Rick took over — breaking in a new boss was *low* on their agendas!

That left only the Provost/VP of Academic Affairs from the officer corps of the past regime. Rick's predecessor recommended interim leaders for the divisions left with vacant VP positions and, after checking these folks out with University System HQ in Atlanta, Rick decided to take his advice in this regard.

Rick's first impression of the Provost was that she was a solid, experienced academician who would be able to coach a newcomer regarding issues of tradition and continuity. There was no officer level position responsible for fundraising. This was not unusual for a relatively small state supported institution. The handwriting was, however, on the wall regarding the need for public colleges to become ever more aggressive in generation of external resources from alumni, friends, employers of graduates, the community and other stakeholders. Rick thought that his relationship building and rainmaking capabilities were a major reason he was selected.

Rick decided to initiate searches to fill the two vacant VP positions — Administration and Student Affairs. He also decided to work with the current Director of Development & Alumni Affairs for a year prior to determining how to proceed there.

Public colleges and universities are usually bound by federal and state recruiting and hiring regulations. These assure equal employment opportunities without regard to race, gender, ethnicity, religion or sexual orientation. They also help preclude nepotism and hiring local favorites who may have strong social backing but be less qualified than others. Sometimes fresh thinking from the outside is desirable and sometimes it's better to "grow your own" talent from within. Usually, a nationally advertised search process is conducted, sometimes using the assistance of a recruiting consultant.

Rick had little experience hiring executive level personnel, so he sent himself to school to learn. At a course on identifying, recruiting, vetting, hiring and retaining quality executives, he learned important new skills. One was how to quiz references of candidates for officer level positions. The challenge is to ascertain character, attitude, resourcefulness, applicable experiences, capabilities and integrity. Bill McElhenney, an alumnus of BRSC who founded and chaired a hugely successful home improvement chain said, *"I'll hire attitude over ability every time!"* Assessing attitude and these other attributes successfully is the trick.

Executive search firms can help here, especially in *identifying* quality candidates. That is as far as Rick counted on them, however. He knew that there was no substitute for taking personal charge of the process of vetting, interviewing and hiring those who would report directly to him.

Checking references provided by a potential recruit is, at the same time, a mandatory and fruitless endeavor. These references have already been screened by candidates to deliver positive feedback. Contacting these references does, however, provide the opportunity to probe them for the names of *other* people who may be in a position to render an opinion about the person being considered.

Rick called this "going three deep." By this he meant, ask the listed references for the names of others they believe are in a position to provide feedback about a person's experiences, capabilities, performance, attitude, integrity, etc. Then ask those second tier people the same question, and so on.

It should go without saying that you should *personally* conduct these telephone interviews when hiring people who will report directly to you. Rick found this to be an onerous, time-consuming function. It was also a critical one. The purpose was to try to ascertain with some confidence whether a candidate has short-comings of which you should be aware. Campus search committees comprised of faculty and staff who perhaps function in this capacity once every two or three years simply aren't sophisticated enough to carry out this critical responsibility effectively. Besides, they don't have to live with the result! A list of open-ended questions to ask references for candidates for executive leadership positions is included in Appendix II. Taking good notes in these conversations is essential. If you are talking to a large number of references, it may be difficult to remember who said what about whom.

Once telephone reference checks have been completed, you are ready to invite candidates for a personal interview. This is a crucial meeting for both parties. It should provide you with an opportunity to determine whether the applicant is a good fit for your organization. A good interview cannot be conducted over a meal. It's too informal. You want the potential leader to feel a little stress so you can evaluate accordingly.

Candidates should also be interviewed by other key players on your team. You need their assessment of the people with whom they are expected to effectively work.

Learning new interview skills also helped Rick to develop a bank of questions to ask candidates for leadership positions during the interview process. These have no correct or incorrect responses. They are designed to elicit from the candidates their approach to various circumstances and for you to learn how they might handle difficult issues in a pressure situation.

In an interview setting it is important to make notes of the candidates' responses as there is, again, a tendency for all the candidates being interviewed to run together in the mind of the interviewer. Plan on inviting candidates for a one and one half hour interview. The open-ended questions are designed to probe people regarding the issues that are critical to the job. Some suggestions may be found in Appendix III. By the time you have carefully checked references and conducted thoughtful interviews you should be ready to make an intelligent choice. In the end, follow your intuition.

Rick established search committees of faculty and staff along with stakeholders from the various departments reporting to each of the VP positions and the college placed advertisements with online networking exchanges and in the *Chronicle of Higher Education,* the weekly trade journal read by almost everyone in America involved in higher education. The ads described the college, its mission and its location. They then went on to list the responsibilities of the VPs along with desirable attributes, experiences and qualifications. They asked applicants to respond by a certain date.

Rick charged the two committees with developing ranking grids based upon the candidates' compliance with the advertised criteria so that each could be scored *quantitatively* on the qualifications important to the college. Each member of the search committees was asked to grade each candidate as applications were received. They planned on 30 to 50 respondents in each search and the ranking system provided a numeric vehicle for comparison.

This approach allowed for identification of the most qualified candidates based on the material submitted in response to the ad. The idea was to winnow down to 10 or 12 highly ranked applicants to include in the first round of interviews.

Rick then asked his office staff (Executive Assistant to the President Madelyn Tavares, a highly qualified and organized mature woman with exceptional interpersonal skills — he was her *third* president! — and a younger secretary, Amy Grossman, with the potential to develop a similar set of qualifications) to reserve a large room at a hotel adjacent to Hartsfield-Jackson Airport in Atlanta. Initial interviews were scheduled at 90 minute intervals over a two day period for each of the VP searches. These initial encounters allowed the search committees to form a first impression regarding the candidates' suitability for the respective positions at Black Rock State.

It took almost three months for the job announcements to appear in the *Chronicle* and on the internet and for interested parties to submit their credentials. The committees then took another six weeks to review the applications, rank the candidates, and identify those rising to the top. By that time, the year-end holiday season was approaching, so the airport interviews were planned for January just before the beginning of spring semester.

Everyone's world was shaken on September 11, 2001. Rick was in his office at about 8:45 AM when Amy Grossman came running in with news gleaned from her internet headliner that an airplane had struck the World Trade Center in New York City. His first thought was that a small private plane must have gotten lost in harbor fog. Amy didn't think so. They all went to take a look at the satellite fed television in the conference room. They had no more than tuned the TV when they watched in horror as the second plane hit the south tower.

They sat in front of the television in stunned silence for some time. Then Rick was shocked into action by the realization that the college might have some students from New York, or at least some with family and friends living there.

He asked his staff to gather the Campus Leadership Team (CLT — the VPs, Deans, Director of Development, the Executive Assistant to the President and the Chair of the Faculty Senate) for an immediate meeting. It didn't take long to decide to cancel classes for the rest of the day. They then planned to gather students in the residence halls in order to provide communication for anyone who might need help contacting home. Almost everyone wanted to touch base with loved ones — it was that kind of emotional rollercoaster.

That evening, the CLT and Rick cruised the residence halls visiting with students. Classes were held per usual the next day and by the evening of

September 12, every residence hall had held a group forum to allow students to discuss events of the day before and to vent their feelings.

Rick decided to invite the few Muslim and Middle Eastern students to the College Home that evening to discuss the issue and to ascertain if any of them had been the recipients of discriminatory behavior. He was glad they did this, as a couple had been approached in a threatening manner and all of them were wary of the situation. He made arrangements with the residence hall staff and faculty to pay special attention to their well-being.

Most faculty members utilized the tragic events of 9/11 as a context for conversation in class about possible causes and repercussions of such horrific acts. On the third night after the catastrophe the Student Senate held a candle light vigil in memory of those killed in New York, Pennsylvania and Virginia. Rick participated by reading some of the text already available from cell phone calls from those trapped at the scene and on airplanes. It was an unforgettable experience for the nation and no less so for an institution of higher learning.

After he believed that the campus had dealt the best it could with the events of 9/11 and the two VP searches were underway, Rick turned his attention to development of a strategic plan for the next three to five years. He needed to put the tragedy behind him and wished for the rest of the campus to do so, as well. This planning process would help the college move as a unit toward a set of overarching goals and objectives.

Rick organized this effort by hosting an off-site retreat for the Campus Leadership Team and the president of the Faculty Senate. The Faculty Senate was the representative governance body consisting of elected members from every organizational unit of the campus. Its main responsibility was development and approval of educational curriculum and coursework. It also conducted peer review of applications for faculty and staff promotional ranks and tenure. And lastly, it was designed to provide a vehicle which could serve as a sounding board for the college administration regarding policy and plans.

Rick had a lot of experience with failed strategic plans. As we learned earlier, Middle Arkansas State University did not have a strategic plan. The MASU president was successful with her own initiatives to obtain funding for new construction and laboratory development; but Rick thought she failed to enlist the rest of the university community in these and other activities because there was no plan where everyone had assigned tasks and was aligned to achieve institution-wide goals.

This shocked Rick since he believed that the main responsibility of the CEO was to constantly scan the environment and anticipate the future so as to be proactive in developing initiatives to cope with changing reality. Rick was fond of saying, "Show me an organization that does not have overarching strategic goals and I will show you an organization adrift!"

He had also been party to strategic planning processes that resulted in well-developed plans which never came to fruition because they were not institutionalized in the form of individual goals and objectives for each organizational unit and employee. Rick was committed to a purposeful, *operational* strategic planning process with measurable goals and outcomes. They started with development of *long range* planning and goals; and, then backed down to the near term. Short term performance was important; but, it was steady progress against long term goals that drove success.

Successful organizations develop plans around a handful of overarching goals. For colleges and universities, these will generally have something to do with admissions selectivity; enrollment; operating cost reduction, revenue generated from fundraising, grant writing and consulting services; new academic degree offerings, and the like. There are usually no more than six to ten of these institutional goals. They can be established at a leadership team retreat over a day or two. Rick planned to host one of these retreats once per year.

He knew that the faculty would probably call for an institutional goal associated with improving student learning. This was certainly an admirable objective. If it was to be an institutional goal, it should have measurable outcomes of some sort. There are plenty of fine texts and studies which attempt to assess learning outcomes and teaching effectiveness. Rick believed it best to leave it to these publications to address student learning. Suffice it to say that it is difficult to measure positive change in learning outcomes. Nevertheless, Rick thought that an institutional goal which created a *learning assessment* initiative was a good move.

Goal statements are action oriented, measurable, and date certain, such as: *"By fall 2005, increase enrollment by 10% over fall 2002."* This provides a target that may be measured and a time frame for completion. It will be easy to determine if the goal has been achieved, or to assess progress along the way.

Another goal might be to reduce overall operating cost from fiscal year (FY) 2002 by 5% by FY 2005. Again, this is easily measured. By the way, some people speak of "cost savings." Costs cannot be *saved*, only *reduced*.

New academic program and curriculum development is essential for most successful higher education institutions. This is due to the dramatic technological changes occurring in every field of study, type of enterprise and work environment. A goal of developing from one to five new academic programs that meet with enrollment success may be appropriate every year, depending on the size of the institution. A market survey regarding enrollment potential and employment opportunities for new academic programs is warranted. Successful marketing has a great deal to do with enrollment, so a goal regarding marketing strategies may be appropriate, as well.

Once the executive team developed institutional goals, each vice president was responsible for establishing *divisional* goals that led to accomplishment of the overarching goals. The VPs accomplished this with their respective team leaders (deans and department heads/directors). Then the deans and directors went through the same exercise with each team, until every organizational entity had departmental goals and objectives that fed into the divisional and then institutional goals.

If an institutional goal is to increase enrollment by a certain percentage, a divisional goal may include increasing enrollment in a specific academic program by a specific amount. If an institutional goal is to add a certain number of new degree offerings every year; then a divisional goal might indicate exactly which new programs the division might develop that will help lead to attainment of this goal.

Departmental goals should then be assigned by department leaders to individuals, with no more than one or two action items per person per year. These individual action items are used to help evaluate individual performance each year. This is a first class way in which to tie rewards to accomplishments which are valued by the institution. It also aligns everyone in the organization and begins moving them in the same direction.

If a divisional goal is to create a new academic degree offering, specific proposal writing and curriculum development activities may be assigned to individual faculty members in a department. Others in this department might be assigned development of specific new course work that would be part of the new degree program. In this way, responsibility for organizational goal achievement is distributed throughout the institution. Everyone has a role to fulfill that leads to institutional goal attainment.

In 2001, BRSC had about 600 employees of whom some 300 were professionals — about 150 faculty and 150 professional staff members. This meant that over 300 action steps toward goal fulfillment were assigned to these folks.

Successful organizations also have vision and mission statements. How else would members know where they are trying to go? A *vision* statement is a single sentence that creates a mental picture of what the organization wishes to be 10 or 15 years into the future. The vision statement should be inspirational and easily remembered. It should rally everyone to the cause. This helps focus members of the organization on the overarching goals. The vision statement should be developed by leaders with input from the greater institution. It creates agreement regarding direction. Members of the organization must believe that achievement of the vision will be worth the effort.

An example of a vision statement might be: "................College is Nebraska's nationally recognized polytechnic institution;" or, "........... University is the premiere research institution of the western US." Goals and objectives are then formulated that drive the organization toward that end.

A *mission* statement sets the context for achieving the vision. It places boundaries on the role of the institution in its environment or system of higher education. It establishes parameters that guide pursuit of the vision. It may be two or three paragraphs long. Most colleges and universities have a specific role that they play in their respective state, region, area of expertise, or system. The mission statement explains the limits of this assigned (or adopted) role. It is the foundation upon which the vision is launched.

Once strategic planning has been accomplished throughout the institution, *annual operating plans* should be developed. These look at the long term goals and select those activities which can be accomplished during the upcoming year that will progress toward achievement of the long range goals.

Annual *operating* plans take into consideration progress against goals for the previous year and set new departmental and individual goals for the new year. They are also used to establish individual goals and objectives for human resource performance evaluation.

In order to develop overarching goals at BRSC, Rick conducted the aforementioned retreat so that the college could develop a few objectives that the entire organization would be charged with achieving. Rick and the CLT were able to accomplish this relatively easily in a two-day off-campus gathering. The institutional goals they developed were as follows.

1. Increase enrollment by 1% per year as compared to fall 2001. (This goal had no time table as they wished it to be operational for the foreseeable future.)
2. Increase average SAT score of entering freshmen by 1% per year until the math and verbal portions total 1100.
3. Initiate two new academic degree programs per year. (Likewise ongoing.)
4. Complete a facilities master plan by June 2003 to project requirements for physical plant enhancement over the next ten years.
5. Increase external fundraising by 10% per year and the college's endowment by 5% per year using 2001 as a basis. (Same ongoing plan.)
6. Enhance the campus life experience for students by the end of spring semester 2005 by creating a non-threatening environment in which all special interest groups may thrive and grow and develop.
7. Develop a campus computing, information and networking environment second to none by the end of calendar year 2003.
8. Develop by June 2003 a student learning assessment program to evaluate trends and support plans for improvement.

The first five and the last of these institutional goals were easily measured. It was resolved to let the Student Affairs professional staff define how goal #6 would be measured and accomplished. They decided to utilize levels of student participation and engagement to assess the success of specific student life offerings. They ultimately set specific participation levels for each student organization and activity as measureable goals.

The Information Technology staff determined that a completely wireless campus environment constituted achievement of goal #7. They agreed to accomplish this within the two year window. The Faculty Senate subsequently took on the assignment of developing tools to measure progress on goal # 8. It utilized valid and reliable commercial instruments to determine student evaluation of teaching effectiveness. They also utilized retention statistics from freshman to sophomore year and graduation statistics for four and six years to assess effectiveness of learning and teaching. Baseline of these statistics then became the benchmark against which progress was assessed.

Prior to adjourning the strategic planning retreat, Rick requested that each participant review the eight institutional goals to determine how his or her area of responsibility would assume a portion of the responsibility for attainment. He then asked each of them to convene their own divisional staff retreat in order to operationalize the goals.

Each was charged with making certain that every professional employee had a defined and measurable action step contribution to make leading to achievement of at least one strategic goal. Faculty and professional staff individual performance reviews were to include an evaluation of accomplishments regarding the assigned action steps. In this way, organizational members became aligned with the institutional goals and goal achievement was actually possible. The Campus Leadership Team could not hope to realize institutional goal completion without the combined contributions of the entire organization.

There were a couple of other concepts that Rick wished the campus to institutionalize. He wanted to consider the *customers* of higher education in any conversation about leadership. Certainly, those who pay for higher education are part of the customer base. This includes parents; taxpayers; federal, state and local governments; donors; and students themselves.

Those who stand to benefit from the successful delivery of higher education services are also key stakeholders. These include students and employers of graduates, to say nothing of society in general. Successful college and university leaders invest a large portion of their time and energy establishing and maintaining positive relationships with all of these stakeholders.

The concept of students as customers is an interesting one. Think of colleges and universities as analogous to a manufacturing or production operation for a moment. Here, as former Georgia Tech Dean John White has pointed out, students are the raw material. They are also the final product. There may be no other enterprise where the customer (the student in this case) is the raw material and the final product; and where the organization is responsible for evaluating the customer's progress every step of the way. At best, the relationship to the higher education student/customer/consumer is a complex one.

That said, the goal should be to make every interaction that customer constituencies have with the institution as hassle-free as possible. We, as a society, are growing less and less tolerant of poor service. Consumers of higher education services are no different. If they conclude that they are being poorly served, they will simply vote with their feet and attend another institution. Higher education customers have many choices. Some BRSC faculty had a difficult time with the concept of students as customers. Given time and enough repetition, most began to come around.

Another of Rick's inaugural issues dealt with meeting management. More time is wasted by people attending inefficient meetings than perhaps any other organizational endeavor. Many folks dread attending meetings. Some take other work, electronic devices or reading material with them, so they can accomplish *something* productive while sitting in poorly planned and led meetings.

When he arrived as president, one of Rick's early obligations at BRSC was to attend an alumni association meeting. The president of the alumni association was a young bank lending officer. The association met monthly to plan its activities and philanthropic support of the college. The alumni president arrived at the meetings, which were held in the evening in order to accommodate working members, with a brief agenda that listed the topics for discussion that evening.

The Director of Development and Alumni Affairs, Jim Antonio who regularly attended these meetings, told Rick that they were out of control and ineffective. The alumni president allowed discussion to ramble wherever anyone in the group might like to take it — frequently it turned into a social gathering. That is all well and good, if that is what the members wished to do; however, most of them complained to Antonio about wasting their time "chasing rabbits" in these gatherings which frequently lasted for over four hours!

No one was willing to confront the alumni president regarding this issue. They wanted someone from the college to do that. This obviously placed Antonio in an awkward position. He suggested to the alumni president that he might like to utilize some of the meeting management tools that were implemented at the college. The alumni president expressed interest, but never subscribed to this approach. As a result, attendance began to dwindle.

Antonio went to a fallback position, and quietly recruited another alumna to run for president of the association. When this person took over, she adopted an approach similar to the one utilized at the college, and participation began to recover.

Rick put the word out that if he encountered a meeting within the college organization that was not carefully planned, he would get up and walked out. He could tell whether a meeting was well planned before attending, as will be related in a moment. People get the message quickly when they think the boss might walk out of their meeting.

Here are some simple steps to assuring that meetings are well planned and productive. First, it goes without saying that every meeting should have an agenda. There are, however, agendas and then there are *AGENDAS*. Here is how to prepare an *AGENDA* and to plan for and conduct a meeting that people will not dread. It's a stretch to imagine that folks will look forward to and enjoy a meeting, so just try to make the meeting one that will be productive, efficient and effective.

To prepare a major league *AGENDA*, first list the topics to be covered. Hopefully, there are no more than 10 or 12 of these. If there are more than 15, it is probably best to plan two separate meetings. The optimum length of a meeting is 60 to 90 minutes. In no case should a meeting last more than two hours. People deserve the opportunity to accomplish something else in their day besides meeting, to say nothing of limited attention spans.

Each agenda item should include a brief description of the topic. This should be enough so that everyone attending will understand the issue. The *AGENDA* should indicate how much time the meeting planner has budgeted to discuss *each* topic. Somewhere between five and 20 minutes ought to be enough. A topic requiring more than 20 minutes to discuss may qualify for its own meeting.

The *AGENDA* should also designate one of the meeting attendees as responsible for leading the conversation regarding each agenda item. Obviously, this should be the person most knowledgeable about the topic, or the one who asked for it to be placed on the agenda.

And finally, the *AGENDA* should express the desired outcome for the discussion of the item. This consists of a short statement of the conclusion to be drawn, decision to be made, or what exactly the discussion is designed to achieve. For example, if an academic department is attempting to develop a new laboratory and there is a budget constraint issue, the agenda description might be, "New Cleedus Phibus Lab;" and the desired outcome might be, "Decide whether or not funding will be available this fiscal year to proceed with development of this lab."

The *AGENDA* should also assign a time keeper. It is this person's responsibility to remind the group how much time has elapsed discussing each item. The time keeper should indicate when there are about two minutes left to finish conversation on each item. This lets attendees know that it is time to address the desired outcome for the item.

A major league *AGENDA* should also designate a scribe. This person will be responsible for preparing minutes of the meeting. Minutes are worth discussing for a moment. There is no need for minutes to include a *transcript* of the meeting. Some meeting minute preparers labor under the false impression that it is their responsibility to capture in writing everything that is said. The idea is to capture the item description and the outcome of the discussion. Scribes who delight in preparing transcripts are really trying to publicize meeting details. Transcripts are, of course, appropriate for legal proceedings and for the minutes of governmental agencies which require public scrutiny. Failing these circumstances, bulleted minutes are adequate.

If the *AGENDA* is properly prepared, it will be relatively easy to create minutes. Simply restate the item description and use one or two sentences to indicate the outcome of the discussion. Minutes will then be only one or two pages of bullet points — much easier with which to deal. The time keeper and scribe responsibilities should be rotated for every meeting, assuming the same players are involved, so no one is over-burdened and so everyone has an opportunity to experience these roles.

Once the *AGENDA* is prepared, the meeting planner adds up the budgeted times allocated for each item to determine total meeting length. The person designated to lead the conversation on each item is expected to arrive at the meeting prepared to undertake that function.

The *AGENDA* should be circulated to the attendees at least two days in advance of the meeting so everyone has an opportunity to prepare. The *schedule* for the meeting (time and place) should be passed to the attendees as early as possible, so folks can plan their calendars.

You may not be able to create excitement over meetings; but, you should be able to minimize apathy and dread towards them. People appreciate the fact that you are attempting to make the most productive use of their time. And, perhaps most important of all, you teach this technique to other members of the organization, thus helping everyone to use their time more efficiently and effectively.

By January 2002 the search committees for the two vacant VP positions were prepared to interview candidates. The initial interviews at the airport went smoothly and on-campus interviews were planned for the finalists in each of the searches.

The finalists were invited to visit during February and March and the search committees made their hiring recommendations to Rick, since he was ultimately responsible for making the selections. He did so and made an offer to a man named David Bradford who was well qualified for the position of VP of Student Affairs. For the position of VP of Administration, he selected a man named Peter Hennessey. Both accepted and were on board by July 1, 2002, the beginning of the next fiscal year.

In the meantime, Rick asked the Chair of the Faculty Senate to place the new Strategic Plan on the agenda for the first Senate meeting of spring semester. He didn't need Senate approval to institute the plan; but, was mindful of the value of an inclusive process and wished the greater campus community to subscribe to it. He was unconcerned regarding its acceptance, since the Faculty Senate chair had participated in the planning and had already relayed its substance to the greater group.

The Strategic Plan contained what the Campus Leadership Team, Faculty Senate chair and Rick believed to be a statement of the obvious challenges facing the college and the goals that would need to be achieved to deal with the realities of the environment. Even though it is leadership's responsibility to study the environment and develop plans for the future, it's always smart to find a role for the greater campus in such an endeavor. Rick was cognizant that, since the campus at large had not participated in the development of these goals, the full Senate needed some time to process them.

Rick commenced his discussion at the Senate meeting by explaining that an increase in enrollment was jugular to the college's well-being, since state funding allocations to the various campuses comprising the public higher education system in Georgia were at the time dispersed based upon enrollment. State allocations comprised about 25% of BRSC's total budget. Tuition and fees paid by students and their families constituted another 25%, residence hall room rental added about 25% and the last 25% came from meal service and other concessions. All told, BRSC was about a $40 million per year enterprise.

It was an amazingly entrepreneurial organization. The food service was operated by a not-for-profit corporation dedicated to the college. It was called BREC — Black Rock Enterprises Corp. Its major function was to provide three meals a day to the campus. Any margin of revenue over costs (there were always several hundred thousand dollars per year of margin) was for use at the president's discretion. In addition to the food service, BREC also ran the campus telephone service for students, the campus cable television service, computer sales and leasing, all the vending machines on campus and the campus book store.

The BREC was a grand way to generate unrestricted money to augment the ever decreasing state allocation. Rick liked to joke, in making the case for the need to raise external resources, that the college used to be state supported, was currently state assisted and would soon be state located — unfortunately, not far from the truth.

Anyway, Rick thought that it was fairly obvious that increasing enrollment (to the extent that classrooms, residence halls and dining facilities were not 100% utilized) would increase revenue from state allocations, from tuition and fees, from residence hall room rental, from food service and from the other services sold to students *without increasing fixed costs!* Not so to some senators. A few began quizzing him in the Senate meeting with regard to the available space for additional students and classrooms.

Rick pointed out that while there might not be excess space in every academic building, there certainly was in some, and that it might be necessary for faculty to walk across campus to teach in a building other than where their office was located. He imagined that it would be beneficial for various departments and educational programs to share space across campus. Faculty and students from different major fields of study would be exposed to alternate settings and people and better integrate, he thought. He could see, however, that some senators were warming to the opposing argument.

"You know it may be that some things will have to change a bit to achieve the goals we're striving to accomplish." Rick said.

"That *you're* striving to accomplish!" a senator shot back. "We're doing just fine the way we're accustomed to operating. Don't you think you should give yourself some time to assess how efficient we are already?"

Rick didn't think the academic side of the campus *was* particularly efficient. Faculty were accustomed to teaching plenty of class *contact* hours, but in too many cases those classes enrolled a small number of students. Academic efficiency should be measured by student *credit* hours (the number of students in each class multiplied by the credit hour value of the class), not class contact hours.

"The bottom line, everyone," he responded, "is that state support for public colleges in Georgia is allocated based upon enrollment. We have additional capacity in many of our academic buildings, in our residence halls and in our dining rooms. We can increase enrollment without increasing costs, for the most part. Therefore, it may be necessary for all of us to be a bit flexible as we move in this direction."

Rick paused and then proceeded to outline for the Senate the remainder of the Strategic Plan. This occurred without further controversy. He closed by asking the Senate to digest the Strategic Plan over the next month and to be ready to discuss it in detail and act upon it at their next meeting.

A few days later the campus grapevine was abuzz. It was thought by some that at the next Faculty Senate meeting there would be an initiative to suggest that the college not grow. The premise was that the reason the institution was of such high quality was its relatively small class sizes. An increase in enrollment, it would be argued, would tend to depersonalize the campus thus leading to erosion of academic quality.

The Provost/VP for Academic Affairs, Margaret Wagenhut, and Rick began to prepare a "position paper" to employ in the next Senate meeting to counter such an argument. Rick wanted to observe Margaret in a stressful debate-type situation, so he asked her to be prepared to lead the administration's participation in the dialogue at the up-coming Senate meeting.

He was not encouraged as he watched her nervously attempting to make the case for enrollment growth. She was a competent thinker with the appropriate building blocks of professional experience, yet Rick thought she lacked the confidence that her arguments would carry the day. Rick found himself breaking in to make a point she had missed or to respond more effectively to the arguments rendered by a few senators.

After extensive debate about the pros and cons of expanding enrollment, the Senate decided to take a vote on whether or not to accept the new Strategic Plan, including the enrollment goal. A small group of senators lobbied for the status quo, but more progressive minds prevailed and the Strategic Plan was accepted by a large majority. Rick was pleased, but also concerned that some were not on board.

Organizational dynamics had always fascinated Rick and he considered himself a fairly astute observer of organizational behavior. He was beginning to be concerned that a small contingent of mal-contents might be working behind the scenes to thwart not just the enrollment initiative, but others, as well. He resolved to seek ways to begin to gain the trust and respect of these folks.

As his first year at Black Rock State College came to a close, Rick concluded that he needed a stronger Provost as academic leader. The deans, academic department chairs and faculty were not pushing hard enough for innovation and that new program development. Rick decided that Margaret Wagenhut was unable to adequately motivate those in her purview. New academic programs were jugular to the college's well-being, if enrollment was going to grow.

Rick requested that Wagenhut instruct the deans and department chairs to initiate this program development, but things didn't transpire quickly enough to satisfy him. Rick didn't believe that he could continue with that situation. At the end of the academic year, he offered her a tenured faculty position for the following year. She was a long term employee in her 60s and he didn't want to cut her adrift. It was hard enough to find a good academic position if you were young.

Margaret apparently had seen the hand writing on the wall, because she graciously accepted his offer. Now he had to search for a new Provost, as well as identify an interim for the upcoming year.

Rick was satisfied, if not overjoyed, with the progress made during his first year on the job. He had led development of a new Strategic Plan; and had hired two new vice presidents to flesh out the leadership of the campus. In addition to these accomplishments, he had worked with the President's Advisory Council to establish a not-for-profit foundation to receive philanthropic gifts to the college. The Black Rock State College Development Fund had earned appropriate classification by the US Internal Revenue Service as a not-for-profit organization capable of accepting gifts that would qualify for donor income tax deduction. This was a critical first step in beginning to build an endowment to enhance campus operations.

One of the college's most successful alumni, J. William McElhenney, had provided a six figure gift (the college's first of that size) to support creation of a bachelor's degree in business administration with a major in entrepreneurship. Bill McElhenney was the founder, CEO and chairman of the board of a wildly successful home improvement store chain. He lived in Atlanta and was generous in his support of causes he viewed as worthy. These included Girls and Boys Clubs, the YMCA, programs designed to prevent teen pregnancies, and the many colleges and universities in the area. His gift was an historic achievement for BRSC and Rick was proud of getting the fundraising initiative off to a good start.

Rick learned during this process, however, that while the BRSC Director of Development was well liked by stakeholders, he didn't bring in much money and lacked credibility with major donors. He decided to search for a VP/Development during the next academic year, as well.

In the meantime, the new VP for Student Affairs, David Bradford, had approached Rick with an idea that he warmed to. Bradford suggested that initiating a football program would be a good recruiting move with regard to student-athletes who might like to continue their playing years at the collegiate level. Dave also believed that football, as much or more than any other sport, added to the social fabric of college life. Students seemed to warm to football games as a rallying point for their social outlets, enthusiasm and support. Football also garnered a good bit of free publicity. Funding the program would be the challenge.

Then the stars seemed to align. Rick received an interesting telephone call in the summer of 2002. It was from Tubby Stallworth who had been the successful head coach of the National Football League Atlanta Falcons for several seasons in the 1980s. Stallworth was now in his 70s and indicated that he was bored in retirement, lived locally and had heard that BRSC might be considering initiation of an intercollegiate football program. If so, he was interested in the coaching job. The prospect of retaining the services of an iconic NFL coach with outstanding name recognition appealed to Rick, so he suggested that Stallworth come to campus to meet with Dave Bradford, John Giordano, BRSC Director of Athletics, and him.

In preparation for this meeting, Rick asked Executive Assistant to the President Mary Tavares, a world-class researcher, to learn all she could about Stallworth's background. It turned out that since his good fortune with the Falcons, Stallworth had done a good deal of job-hopping toward the end of his storied career, some of it on short notice. He always seemed to be searching for greener pastures. This lit a caution light in Rick's mind.

The meeting took place in early fall semester of 2002. After ascertaining that Coach Stallworth could be retained for a reasonable salary not out of line with the other coaches on campus and discussing guidelines for a new football program, Rick asked Bradford and Giordano to draw up an agreement between the college and Coach which would outline his responsibilities. These were to include interaction with the news media, recruiting student-athletes, obtaining commitments from eight or 10 teams in NCAA, Div. IAA (now the Football Championship Series — FCS) to play in the fall of 2003, and development of the necessary practice and playing facilities.

The college already had a small soccer stadium which would suffice for football until funds were available for something grander (which it was understood might take several years to realize). Rick also thought that this endeavor would give him a good opportunity to observe both Dave Bradford and John Giordano in an expansive role.

Stallworth assured them that BRSC was a perfect college and Clayton a perfect location for him to end his career. He was on board by December 2002.

Jim Antonio, Director of Development, advised Rick early in his tenure that BRSC had a high profile celebrity alumnus in Junior Samples who was a successful race car driver in the elite NASCAR Winston Cup series. Junior drove the No. 67 Dodge sponsored by Southern States Motor Oil. Jim called Junior's publicist and obtained a commitment for Junior to meet with them at the fall 2001 Winston Cup race at Atlanta Motor Speedway in Hampton, GA about 20 miles south of Atlanta. They drove down together for the Sunday race and met with Junior in the office of his race car hauler inside the paddock area reserved for drivers and their teams.

Junior was a personable young man in his early 30s who was enjoying life as a sports hero in a grand venue. Rick assessed from their conversation that Junior was still young enough to be building his wealth, as opposed to having such deep pockets that he would instantly make a major gift to Black Rock State.

Samples did, however, offer to arrange for them to bring BRSC alumni and others with whom they were building relationships to races. He provided them with NASCAR team credentials such that they could enter the paddock and pit areas before and during races. This turned out to be an *immensely* popular and unique experience of which potential donors were most appreciative. It was an unbeatable opportunity to spend a great deal of one-on-one time with folks with the ability to help BRSC.

Junior introduced them to many of the other Winston Cup drivers and team owners. They also attended the pre-race drivers' meetings conducted by NASCAR. They *all* (even Sally) became race fans! Over the next several years, sometimes with spouses and sometimes without, Rick and his staff hosted (thanks to Junior) groups of alumni at races in Atlanta, Charlotte, Bristol, Rockingham, Darlington, Richmond and Martinsville. It was a bonanza for BRSC and their fundraising endeavors.

Late in the spring of 2002, Rick was approached by the president of the Rabun County United Way and asked to serve on its board of directors. He had always been a believer in the approach with which United Way organizes communities in support of effective social services. Its positive impact enhances the quality of life for all who participate in the good work of its agencies. And it reduces fundraising overhead of the agencies under its umbrella.

Rick agreed to serve and began nine years of involvement in this worthy cause. He had no idea at the time how this participation would benefit him and the college. He developed relationships with a large number of local folks who he might not have otherwise encountered. Many of these were in a position to assist the college in its endeavors. Sally and he also made wonderful friends through this United Way experience. It was impossible to have close friendships with those in the BRSC organization. The job always got in the way. They were fortunate have the United Way vehicle as an alternative.

Sally had a hard time adjusting after her arrival in early December 2001. She had uprooted herself, sold the home in which they had raised their children, closed down her consulting business, left friends of long standing and moved to a new place where she knew no one and where she seemed to lack a life outside that of her husband.

It was a difficult transition for her. She felt like she was living in a fish bowl with no identity of her own separate from Rick's. Her first months in Clayton were not happy ones for her.

Rick tried to help her search for an initiative in which to contribute in a meaningful way. He arranged for her to attend President's Advisory Council meetings. In this way, he hoped, she would be able to stay abreast of emerging issues on campus and he would benefit from her wise and knowledgeable counsel. He was naïve. The campus didn't trust her involvement. If she attended a meeting without Rick, some assumed that she was just "eyes and ears" for him. Besides, as she quickly apprised him, she needed to find her own niche. She did, but it took the better portion of three difficult years.

Chapter Six

The Honey Fades from the Moon

> *"If your actions inspire others to dream more, learn more, do more and become more, you are a leader."* —John Quincy Adams

At the beginning of the 2002-03 academic year the new VPs took up their positions on the BRSC Campus Leadership Team. Dave Bradford was a student-centered student affairs executive. He had experience as a minority affairs coordinator on a good sized campus and was bright and personable. He had not had experience leading large numbers of people or managing large sums of money. He was 50 years of age.

Peter Hennessey came to BRSC from the position of comptroller at a small private liberal arts college. Although he was relatively young at age 42, he seemed to possess all the necessary building blocks to succeed in a leadership position in the financial arena. He too had not had a lot of experience with large numbers of people reporting to him. He was well prepared regarding the fiscal affairs of a college, but had no experience leading physical plant operations, information technology, food service or human resources all of which reported to his position. He also had no experience with publicly funded higher education but Rick was hopeful that managing the resources of a public institution would be easier than wrestling to balance the budget of the private college where he served as comptroller. Rick was confident that the existing seasoned staff in the business, physical plant, dining services and IT offices would provide the support that Hennessey required until he got his feet on the ground.

Rick appointed a popular dean who was nearing retirement to the position of Interim Provost. Ben Whitchurch had been Dean of Business Administration for five of his close to 40 years at BRSC. He was solid and honest with no hidden agendas. Rick trusted him to fill in as they searched for an innovative officer to lead academic affairs.

As his second year commenced Rick, with two new lieutenants in place, was looking forward to making great progress. He hadn't considered the potential for a change in state leadership that occurred in the fall of 2002. A Republican was elected governor of the State of Georgia for the first time since the 19th century. Republicans achieved majorities in both houses of the state legislature, as well. Rick guessed that this might mean a more conservative Board of Regents and a more conservative approach to state funding for higher education.

It was obvious that state tax revenues would be reduced for the current fiscal year, due to the negative economic impact of 9/11. When this type of fiscal challenge occurs, governors and state legislatures act to protect first health care for their citizens and next K-12 education. Allocation of scarce resources to higher education is also apt to play second fiddle to transportation, economic development and other state agencies for one simple reason. Public higher education is one of the few state agencies capable of generating revenue for itself.

It is not unusual for state governments to reduce allocations to public institutions of higher learning and then to raise tuition and fees, thus transferring the burden of cost for their operation from the taxpayer to the consumer. That is where the higher education institutions of the University System of Georgia found themselves at the beginning of 2003.

The Georgia Legislature meets each year starting the second week in January for 40 working sessions. It generally wraps up in mid-April. The last legislative action is usually the establishment of the budget for the following fiscal year. It then takes the University System some time to authorize budgets for each of the over 30 campuses.

The annual budget for Black Rock State College was reduced by 10% for the fiscal year beginning July 1, 2003 and no tuition increase was granted. Needless to say, this created a stressful situation for the college. Since 60% of faculty and professional staff were tenured and since the remainder had already signed employment contracts in the spring of 2003 for the next fiscal year, it was impossible to achieve reduction in cost by reducing the workforce, except through natural attrition (retirements and resignations).

The Campus Leadership Team (CLT) and Rick went about identifying areas that might offer the opportunity to reduce costs. It was a taxing operation but by leaving vacant those personnel positions that became open due to natural attrition and cutting back on some laboratory development initiatives, they were able to squeak through the year.

Rick assumed that the next fiscal year would not be any better, so he asked the CLT to begin to develop a Reorganization Plan to deal with another round of budget cuts for fiscal year (FY) 2004-05. Since over 70% of the college's budget was comprised of the salaries and fringe benefits of employees, it became necessary to try to eliminate positions where possible.

To do this, the CLT focused on academic and extracurricular programs that were undersubscribed by students. They looked at student/faculty ratios, student-credit hours (the number of students in each class multiplied by the credit hour value of the class and summed for all classes taught by each faculty member) taught per faculty member in each program of study, square feet of building space cleaned per custodian, acres of campus real estate cared for per maintenance employee, number of students served per residence hall advisor, and the like. These they compared to like data for similar institutions available from the System Office in Atlanta and from other state operated systems of public higher education.

In this way, they were able to begin to uncover opportunities for downsizing the work force. Rick knew that implementing such a plan was going to be challenging. Eliminating jobs was never pleasant, especially when some of those affected were good, loyal, long term employees. Nonetheless, he asked to be placed on the agenda for a Faculty Senate meeting in spring 2004 in order to roll out a draft of this Reorganization Plan.

Rick decided to do this in a couple of stages, as he had done with the Strategic Plan. The first time he addressed the subject with the Senate, he spoke in generalities about the state budget situation and the need to reduce operating costs. He mentioned no one by name, of course, and didn't even attempt to point to any likely departmental candidates. Those present were, however, astute enough to realize whose ox was about to be gored.

A senator rose to oppose a targeted approach to addressing the challenge. "Why don't all departments agree to take an equal percentage cut across the board?" she posed. "That way, no single area of the college will be dramatically affected in a negative manner."

"We have some inefficiencies which we need to address." Rick explained. "We don't want to unnecessarily disrupt programs that are heavily subscribed by students in order to save some that are not."

"Well, that's easy enough for you to say." snapped this senator. "You're not long term here. We're family and this is the way we've handled this kind of challenge in the past. You're supposed to look out for our best interests."

"I thought that we were all here to look out for the best interests of our clientele, our students." Rick argued. "I don't think that an across-the-board reduction is in best interests of students." A few others engaged in the debate and the session ended soberly as the hand writing appeared to be on the wall.

After Ben Whitchurch took over as interim Provost and VP/Academic Affairs, Rick initiated a search to fill this position on a permanent basis. By Spring 2003, the search committee charged with identifying candidates and he had agreed on an inspiring hire. The person was Dean of Faculty at a small private liberal arts college. She had about 25 years of experience teaching and leading academic enterprises. Her name was Naomi Perkins and she proved to be a strong leader with the courage to deal effectively with both budget reality and the people affected by it. She also did a superlative job of implementing the Strategic Plan. Rick was thrilled at the successful conclusion of this process.

New football coach Tubby Stallworth had come onboard in late fall semester 2002. He began an intensive recruiting campaign. Since he was an iconic figure in Georgia due to his successful years coaching the Atlanta Falcons, this was an easy undertaking for him. He visited with high school coaches from the northern Atlanta suburbs to the North Carolina and Tennessee borders. By March he had assembled a strong group of players committed to attending Black Rock State in the fall of 2003. These athletes were, for the most part, players whose size, ability or academic background did not render them attractive to NCAA, Bowl Championship Series (BCS) football programs. Rick was convinced that next to none of these recruits would have been interested in BRSC had it not been for the opportunity to: a) play football; and b) be coached by Tubby Stallworth.

The newspapers — both in Atlanta and in northeast Georgia — covered Stallworth's exploits about once per week. What a lovely gift of *free* publicity! Nothing like having a celebrity in our midst.

Coach Stallworth and AD John Giordano were able to cobble together a game schedule for the fall of 2003 playing two-year colleges and NCAA junior varsity teams the first year. This was of great interest to the sports media and it resulted in terrific exposure for the college. Stallworth also held on-campus tryouts in spring semester 2003 for current students who had played football in high school and who might be interested in competing for the upcoming season.

Rick learned during spring semester that Stallworth had been commuting to campus from his home in Atlanta over 100 miles away. This made him wonder about the level of Stallworth's commitment. Rick had hoped that he might rent an apartment or even move permanently to Clayton.

He asked Dave Bradford to meet with AD Giordano and Stallworth to discuss support for the football program and to assess Stallworth's level of satisfaction. Dave came away from the encounter worried about Stallworth's expressed concern regarding the small number of athletic grants that the college was able to offer to football athletes this first year. This, even though that very topic had been covered in initial discussions between the parties before Coach came onboard. It was now May 2003.

The main bone of contention for Coach Stallworth centered around his desire for more tuition waivers and campus jobs for football players. Dave reminded Coach that decisions regarding allocation of these resources between each sport were the responsibility of the Athletics Director and that he should discuss this issue with Giordano, if he believed that he was being short-changed. Dave sensed that everything was not running as smoothly as he would like; but, he could find no real areas where he believed that the college was not living up to its agreements with Stallworth regarding support for the football program.

Rick ruminated on Bradford's thoughts. He could not bring himself to believe that Coach did not want the football program to succeed as badly as he did.

"Surely, Giordano will explain these issues to Coach!" he posited to Dave. "Let's you and I meet with them both and try to get all their concerns aired and resolved. Maybe the three of us can get Coach to understand the fiscal constraints with which we are dealing."

The four met in late May. Rick started things off by congratulating both men for initiating the football program and for the recruiting successes thus far.

"I'd feel a whole lot better if I had 10 or 12 more grants to tie down some really good looking out-of-state athletes." pleaded Coach.

"That's a revenue loss that the college would have to make up in its budget, Coach. John, you have an allocation of grants for all of the athletic programs. Can you afford more for football?" Rick queried the AD.

"Not without short changing another program. I don't recommend doing that." he responded.

"I'd have a hard time justifying cut-backs over and above those already prescribed in the Reorganization Plan in order to provide more grants for a new football program. We're just going to have to wait until the state budget is in a better position before we add more aid for athletes." Rick tried to explain. "Coach I'm sorry, you're going to have to live with the grants you've got for this year." Thus, the meeting ended. Rick found himself unsatisfied with the encounter.

In June, after a late May commencement exercise, Sally and Rick took a couple of weeks' vacation at their Ozark Mountain retreat. Their children joined them and it was a refreshing breather for all of them.

Upon returning to campus, Rick asked Dave Bradford to give him an update regarding the football program. Student athletes were due to arrive on campus in mid-August and he was concerned about the stability of the undertaking. Dave seemed relaxed about it. He advised that Coach Stallworth was back in Atlanta awaiting the arrival of the athletes.

"I'm nervous about Stallworth, Dave. He's been concerned about the small number of tuition waivers we've been able to allocate for football this first year and he's been known to bolt on short notice. Why don't you quietly identify some assistant head coaches in the southeast who you think might like to take over a new program, just in case?" Rick suggested to Bradford.

Dave was surprised and a bit chagrined that he hadn't done so already. Rick decided to wait things out. Maybe, he thought, I'm just being paranoid.

Chapter 6

The Nedics spent the weekend of August 9 and 10 in Atlanta taking in a Braves game and an Elton John concert at the Fox Theatre. They returned home on Sunday evening to find a message on the phone from John Giordano and several from the sports media wanting a comment on Tubby Stallworth's resignation as football coach!

Dave Bradford had left the day before to visit his daughter in California. Rick reached him on his cell phone and learned that Bradford knew nothing of the latest development.

"Alright Dave, I'll get ahold of Giordano and we'll start looking for a new coach." Rick decided not to interrupt the VP's vacation.

"I'll come right back, if you like." Bradford offered.

"No don't bother. This will give me an opportunity to work with and get to know Giordano a bit better. You've had him developing a list of possible candidates haven't you?" Rick stated.

"Yes, he should be prepared." Dave responded.

"Ok, I'll take it from here and keep you posted." Rick rang off.

Rick called John Giordano and asked him to line up coaching candidates for them to interview as soon as possible. He was in his office on campus on Monday morning August 11 when he received a telephone call from Roman Girardi, President of Calhoun State College in Calhoun, Georgia. Girardi was a casual friend and colleague.

Much to Rick's amazement, Girardi informed him that Tubby Stallworth had visited Calhoun State last Friday afternoon and Saturday to discuss a deal wherein he would move there to start a new football program! Rick's jaw dropped.

"I'd like to consider hiring Stallworth, if he's leaving you." exclaimed Girardi.

"I don't have anything official to indicate that he's leaving, Roman." Rick responded icily. "I'm not certain that I even want him around here after exhibiting this kind of behavior. Why would you?"

"Well like you, I think that adding football will increase enrollment." Girardi offered.

"It's a free country, Roman. You're welcome to him." Rick declared. "Just make certain that he leaves with us the athletes that he recruited for Black Rock State!"

Rick hung up. To Hell with you, Girardi! Strong letter to follow, he thought.

It turned out that with the media all over the Stallworth resignation, assistant coaches from other colleges were ringing the phone off the hook in the Athletics Dept. There was an eager young assistant head football coach at the University of North Georgia in nearby Dahlonega who was well qualified and enthusiastic at the prospect of joining BRSC as head coach. He was on board and meeting with the incoming players the next day.

The fledgling football program played eight games in its first year, winning two. Rick was amazed that it did *that* well considering the fact that Stallworth took as many good athletes as possible with him when he left. *Thanks again, Roman!*

Sally continued to struggle to find her niche. Rick didn't fully appreciate how much his high profile position impacted her. She felt that she had no life separate from his — no identity other than that of wife of the president in a small college town.

One of the benefits of the University System of Georgia was a complete physical examination every year for presidents and their spouses. Sally was finishing hers when her physician, obviously aware of her state of mind, asked if she was depressed.

"Oh, I think I am a bit." admitted Sally. "I feel like I need to get a life. Whenever anyone asks me what I do, I don't have much to say. I'm feeling like a fifth wheel!" she disclosed uneasily in spite of her own background in psychology.

"I think you *have* a life, Sally." said her doctor. "I think you just need a retort."

"A retort? Like what?" smiled Sally.

"How about, kiss my ass!" came the response.

That was the turning point for Sally. She seemed more and more lighthearted, after that. Sometimes being a good physician is all about interacting with your patient!

It hadn't taken Rick the two years that he had now been at BRSC to realize that poultry farming was a *huge* enterprise in northeast Georgia; but, it did take him that long to begin to figure out a role for the college in this fascinating business. Georgia annually produces more pounds of broilers than any other state in the nation. The rolling hills of the northeastern portion of the state are dotted with chicken coops. Coops does not really describe these long narrow, low slung buildings with a large feed bin and automatic spreader in the middle. Baby chicks are supplied once every eight or so weeks — thousands per coop! Chicken feed is provided at the same time.

Six weeks later, the chicken hauler returns to collect the fully grown broilers. The farmer is paid based on the weight ratio of the broilers to the feed consumed. The farmer then has two weeks in which to clean and maintain the coop and feed spreader for the arrival of the next batch of chicks. It's an interesting and lucrative business.

When Ben Whitchurch took over as Interim Provost, Rick asked him to look into development of a specialized degree in Poultry Business Administration. This was relatively easy to do, since all of the foundational business courses were available in the BRSC generic BBA. Rick was certain that this would be a winner with both prospective students and employers/farmers. Gainesville, Georgia to the south about 40 miles was home to several national chicken processing chains and to the large chicken feed producers. He knew this new degree program would be a winner there, as well!

As he entered his third year at Black Rock State, Rick was ill at ease with the challenges that lay ahead associated with implementing the Reorganization Plan and the resultant downsizing of the college workforce. He was pleased though, with progress against the new Strategic Plan, with the new VPs of Student Affairs and Administrative Affairs and with the football initiative.

Chapter Seven

Plans Begin to Coalesce

"Good fortune is what happens when opportunity meets with planning."
—Thomas A. Edison

After the football soap opera — *"As the Football Bounces!"* — and as Rick was preparing for the opening of his third academic year at Black Rock State College, he turned his attention to the Reorganization Plan. Downsizing an organization is never an easy proposition. With another fairly dramatic reduction in budget to be faced, the Campus Leadership Team and Rick had developed an approach to accommodating fiscal reality by doing away with academic programs and student activities that were undersubscribed.

This involved terminating some tenured faculty who were teaching in academic programs that had few student majors and for which the academic deans, the Provost and he agreed were probably not going to recover adequate enrollment. This was particularly onerous, since some of the faculty involved were solid, long-term contributors.

One faculty member sent her teenaged children to request a meeting with Rick to question why it was that their mother was losing her job. Rick debated about accepting such an unprofessional approach. He finally decided that the humane thing to do was to agree to meet, knowing that no amount of explanation would satisfy his inquisitors. It was a difficult encounter and in the end Rick was glad he had conducted it. It tended to prove the point that it's the little things that count in building trust and respect.

Between layoffs and leaving vacant positions unfilled during FY 2003-04 the college downsized again, this time by about 5% of its then approximately 575 employees. There were not a lot of employment opportunities in and around Clayton for folks who did not wish to uproot their families. Most of those affected behaved like the professionals that they were. Some were even hired back in a year or two, as other vacancies were created by resignations and retirements.

At the start of the 2002-03 academic year, Rick had asked the campus leadership corps to operationalize the Strategic Plan. Each department leader was requested to gather the members involved to dissect the Strategic Plan in order to identify those actions which the given department could undertake and which would contribute to the achievement of institutional goals.

These action steps were then assigned to individual employees (faculty and professional staff alike) as part of their responsibilities for the year (over and above their regular job responsibilities) and against which they would be evaluated thereafter. In this way, each member of the organization's faculty and professional staff had at least one strategic action step, in addition to their normal contribution, for which they were responsible. This process helped align everyone with the overarching college goals and objectives. And each understood that rewards would be tied to successful attainment thereof. It was a simple yet elegant approach that worked exceedingly well.

One of the college's strategic goals dealt with increasing external fundraising and enhancing the endowment. Fundraising is an area with easily measured outcomes. Dollars raised, percent of alumni participating in an annual campaign, and trends of endowment growth are several parameters which may be assessed with little effort.

Rick was not satisfied with the progress in the development/fundraising purview. He found a fit for the director of this area, Jim Antonio (he was a long-term member of the organization) in the business office. He then proceeded to search for new leadership for this vital function.

Rick knew that the ideal chief development officer would have superior interpersonal skills, an intimate knowledge of the college, and successful experience raising pots of money. He also decided that it would be impractical to expect to find someone who had all three of these attributes, so he decided to settle for two of them.

Budget constraints made it difficult to justify bringing in a professional fundraiser from outside the college, especially with no position vacancy since he had arranged for the prior director to remain at the college in the business office. So, Rick began an internal search for a member of the existing organization who was reasonably well seasoned at the college with exceptional interpersonal skills and who was interested and assertive.

He found such a person in a man who had been at BRSC for almost 20 years, first as a faculty member teaching history and then as an administrator responsible for student development — the arm of the college that works with students to maximize success rates (retention and graduation) by providing support services such as counseling, tutoring, study skills, time management, and the like. The college conducted an internal search for the position of VP/Advancement and at the end of fall semester 2003 and Rick appointed

Robert (Bob) Carlisle to the position. He set about building a board of directors for the newly formed Black Rock State College Development Fund. The purpose of the fund and its board was to generate ever-increasing annual gifts to the college and to build its endowment which currently stood at less than $1 million.

With Carlisle and the new Provost Naomi Perkins in place, along with Dave Bradford in Student Affairs and Peter Hennessey in Administrative Affairs, Rick *finally* had, after three long years, an effective team of college officers. He turned his attention to the business of creating new academic programs designed to attract and prepare 21st century students for 21st century jobs. These programs would help build enrollment which would lead to a stronger fiscal stance.

It's worth discussing for a moment why an organization will follow a leader even when he or she is instituting unpopular and difficult measures. Leaders with high visibility must be able and willing to withstand "the slings and arrows of outrageous fortune." Rick's experience was that people are forgiving of leaders who accept responsibility, apologize when appropriate, and move forward with renewed sense of humility, making new mistakes everyday; but never the same one twice. People appreciate a leader who, after accepting responsibility for a negative outcome, does not make the same mistake again and who makes adjustments to plans to compensate for undesirable outcomes. After all, exhibiting the same behavior or pursuing the same agenda over and over and expecting a different result really *is* the definition of insanity, isn't it?

A leader who demonstrates the ability to learn and change and grow will be much more apt to meet with positive results. The successes Rick enjoyed in his leadership roles he attributed almost entirely to a willingness to assess outcomes, to share credit and accept responsibility, to adjust plans and to move forward with a renewed understanding of self and the human and organizational dynamic.

Rick found that accepting responsibility for the outcomes he produced generated large amounts of trust and respect among the members of the BRSC organization. Trust and respect are hard-earned qualities. We garner them one day at a time, one person at a time, day-in and day-out by behaving with integrity. This may be accomplished, in part, by treating *others* with trust and respect.

Rick always assumed that people were trustworthy until they prove themselves otherwise. Yes, he was occasionally burned by this approach, but not often. Most people want to be trusted and when they are, they return the honor. Yes, honor! How could anyone honor you more than by trusting you?

Chapter Eight

Friendraising and Fundraising

> "There is a bank that credits your account each morning with $86,400. It carries no balance from day to day. Every evening, it deletes whatever part of the balance you failed to use during that day. What would you do? Draw out all of it every day, of course!
> "Each of us has such a bank. Its name is time. Every morning, it credits us with 86,400 seconds. Every night, it writes off as lost whatever of this we have failed to put to good purpose. It carries no balance. It allows no overdraft."
> —Source unknown.

By the beginning of Rick's fourth year, the new academic programs that had been established over the last couple of years began to pay off in terms of increased enrollment and the associated additional revenue generation. The BBA in Poultry Business Management was at the forefront. These new programs of study were thoroughly researched before they were proposed to assure that they would provide students with knowledge, skills and abilities required by employers in the region.

With increased enrollment came increased tuition revenue, increased state allocation (which was based on enrollment), increased room rental, increased food service revenue, and the other monies generated by increased student population — campus book store revenue, vending monies, telephone service fees, sale and lease of computing equipment (which varied depending on academic program of study), and cable television service fees.

The politics of the change in leadership of the State of Georgia from Democrat to Republican control at the beginning of 2003 brought about changes in the upper echelons of the University System. New Regents were appointed by the Republican Governor and his new appointees were understandably sympathetic to his agenda for the System.

Also, the Chancellor of the University System, Mike Talbot, who Rick had come to admire and respect, was eased out and a new appointment was made whose background was as a corporate CEO. This led to enhanced initiatives for funding from federal (also Republican controlled at the time) and state government agencies.

Bob Carlisle took over his new responsibilities as VP/Advancement. He and Rick spent a good deal of time together as they prepared for a focused fundraising endeavor. The college needed a strong alumni relations program to host gatherings designed to connect graduates with their alma mater. The Director of Alumni Affairs reported to Bob. They planned annual alumni events in eight or 10 cities around the southeastern US where there were concentrations of BRSC graduates.

The college, of course, was interested in identifying and cultivating relationships with alumni who had enjoyed financial success in their careers and who were at the stage of their lives (over age 55) where they might consider a major gift to the college. Bob asked the Director of Alumni Affairs to assemble a list of these folks, as best she knew them. They sent this list to a prospect research consultant to assess their wealth.

The consultant checked public data bases against the list. These data bases included real estate holdings listed through property tax assessments, membership on corporate boards of directors for companies listed on the stock exchanges, Security & Exchange Commission listings of corporate officers, contributions to political action committees which must be publicly recorded, professional directories, news articles, search engines and the like.

It was the goal to develop positive relationships with these alumni and employers of graduates. People give their money to those they know and trust.

Rick had always found it easy to ask others for their money for two reasons. First, the cause he represented was a worthy one — a college that provided a comprehensive and useful education to large numbers of people. Rick was helping to make the college more efficient and effective by virtue of the strategic, operational and reorganization plans. With decreasing state tax allocations, additional resources were needed to provide scholarships for needy students, to support new academic program development, to fund faculty chairs, for laboratory equipment and for physical plant enhancement.

Secondly, Rick believed that when he asked people for money for a worthy cause he was providing them with an opportunity to feel good about themselves. This he knew from his own philanthropic endeavors supporting causes in which he and Sally strongly believed. There is elation in watching your support being put to good use.

At the end of the academic year, they managed to obtain a commitment from the new Chair of the University System Board of Regents to speak at commencement. This gave Rick an opportunity to show her around the campus, to expose her to some of the college's more impressive initiatives and laboratories, and to enhance his working relationship with her.

Rick labored incessantly to foster visits by Regents and members of the University System administrative leadership staff in order to develop positive relationships with them. These laid the groundwork for support of the college's mission and programs that the institution would need going forward.

They did the same with state and federal legislative delegations. Rick made frequent trips to Atlanta and Washington to visit (read: lobby) these folks in support of the college and its various initiatives.

During the course of their third year at BRSC, Sally found her niche. The Director of Student Activities whose job it was (amongst many other things) to recruit faculty and staff members to serve on a volunteer basis as advisors to student clubs and organizations, called Sally indicating that she was at her wits end in attempting to recruit someone suitable to be advisor to the Rainbow Union, the lesbian, gay, bisexual, transgender (LGBT) student organization. Sally was pleased to be *asked* to do this, since her attempts at involvement at BRSC had been met with skepticism.

Sally suggested that she attend a meeting of the group to assess their reaction to her participation. She sat quietly through the meeting and gathered as much information as she could without probing and causing stress. At the end of the meeting, the student leader of the group turned to her and questioned as follows.

"Ms. Nedic, why is the president's wife interested in RU?"

Sally was all too aware that she might be perceived as a spy in their midst. She responded. "Well, you look to me like a group that could use some clout and I sleep with the president!"

She always knew exactly the right thing to say. Those students were hers ever after. They moved their meetings off campus to the College Home, so as to be as inconspicuous as possible.

The first couple of years in her role as advisor to RU were not easy for Sally. Some faculty and staff members thought it outrageous that the spouse of the president would "stoop" to advising such a group. She endured a good bit of anonymous hate mail which only strengthened her resolve to support these youngsters. She had found her calling and she became an icon for these students and for gay rights in general. She achieved such notoriety in this role that the American Association of State Colleges and Universities (AASCU) asked her to speak on the subject at their annual meeting.

Rick utilized an hour every Friday afternoon to conduct seminars with the college's leadership corps (VPs, deans, department chairs, directors and Faculty Senate Executive Committee) to teach techniques which he believed would help them and BRSC become more efficient and effective. Time management was an issue with which he had struggled throughout his career. He had learned some techniques that he wished to share with those who were in leadership positions.

Time management is really *self*-management. No one can manage your time for you; only you can do this. Each of us has the same amount of time to invest. Some people, however, are able to accomplish more with their time than others. Rick believed that there were some good tools that maximize effective use of time.

The first is the phrase, "Please handle." Rick delegated everything he possibly could. Most requests from boards of directors or others to whom he had reported, or from key customers, required input from people in the organization who knew more about a specific issue than he did.

If the chairman of the board was interested enough in a topic to inquire about it, you can bet that Rick wanted to learn about it also. When such a request came across his desk, he asked an expert staff member to brief him. After the briefing, Rick asked for a draft response (assuming one was called for) for his review and eventual use.

Too many CEO's falter because they insist on actually trying to *perform* some work. The job of the CEO, for the most part, is to *orchestrate*, not to perform. By delegating, Rick avoided becoming a bottleneck.

Next, he learned how to read 10,000 words per second. Fortunately, this was easier than it sounds. In order to read 10,000 words per second, you carefully read the *subject* of each document that passes over your desk. If, in reading the subject, you do not conclude that it is essential that you be knowledgeable about the topic, place the document "in the circular file" — the waste basket. Or, if you think you should have some knowledge about the issue, ask your assistant to read it and to brief you. If you think that someone else in the organization should become knowledgeable about the topic, use the "please handle" technique. It should go without saying that there are *plenty* of lengthy documents that the CEO needs to study carefully.

For a while, Rick kept the documents that he chose *not* to read, concerned that the chancellor, a board member or an important client or media representative would expect him to be knowledgeable about them. This *never* happened, and he soon stopped saving them at all.

Sir Winston Churchill once expressed this approach to speed reading better than anyone. "The very length and breadth and volume of this document guard it against all risk of being read!" he stated. Amen.

Thirdly, have your assistant or an appointments secretary keep your calendar. It may be disconcerting at first to turn the planning of your life over to someone else. It is, however, a huge relief not to have to worry with this. Make certain that you establish guidelines for your assistant to utilize. You may wish to establish inviolate hours during each day to return phone calls, read mail, work on a specific project, think deeply about current challenges, or just to stroll about the campus. All you have to do when your assistant keeps your calendar is to show up at the appropriate place and time prepared to discuss whatever the conversation demands. Make it the responsibility of your assistant to assure that you *are* prepared for these conversations.

Many CEOs wish to maintain an open door policy for meetings requested by members of the organization and for customers. Rick believed this to be an appropriate approach. It is, however, essential to have a "screener" (usually your assistant) whose job it is to handle those issues which do not *require* your attention. This will include most of the issues with which people wish you to deal!

Many folks think that they have a better chance of their issues being resolved in their interests, if the CEO handles it personally. Most issues are best handled by the most knowledgeable person in the organization, usually *not* the CEO. The job of the CEO is to scan the horizon, to develop strategies for dealing with environmental challenges, and to "close deals." A good office staff is essential and should be highly valued. It should do everything else.

A screener who can deftly handle difficult conversations with employees, stakeholders or students is worth his or her weight in gold. This person should be someone who can de-escalate difficult situations and reach a satisfactory resolution with the visitor or caller. This is not an easy job, nor one for the faint of heart. It requires application of patience, courtesy, self-control, and resourcefulness. The screener must be able to think quickly on his or her feet while in the throes of stressful encounters. A good screener will be able to handle over 90% of the requests to see you.

There are also issues where you as CEO may be the "court of last resort." In other words, you may need to adjudicate the issue after other members of your staff have made their associated decisions/recommendations. In this scenario, it is important for you not to be pulled into the fray too early. Your assistant can advise the petitioner that you are not getting involved at this time, as there is an appeal process which involves your review. Members of the organization and students need to understand that there are policies that the institution follows regarding human resource, academic and other issues.

For the less than 10% of issues that your screener deems necessary for you to handle, he or she should understand the situation fully so as to best prepare you for the encounter. This also requires a good bit of diplomacy, as many folks wish to share their issue *only* with the CEO. The screener's job is to convince them that there is greater likelihood of meeting with you or reaching resolution, if the screener has all the facts. Again, not a job for the timid.

The screener should also monitor your conventional mail and your email, and everyone in the organization should know this is your modus operandi. People will then know that others than you will be seeing their correspondence. The screener can handle the vast majority of these contacts. In the end, the idea is to keep you from becoming bogged down in "administrivia."

Your assistant should keep a "tickler (also called follow-up or suspense) file" for you. A tickler or follow-up file is a folder (paper or electronic) where you and your assistant file items that need attention at some future date. A typical follow-up file will list days of the month for two months, i.e. 61 days of dates, numbered 1-30 and then repeating 1-31. If you want to revisit an issue in two weeks' time, it goes into the file folder marked with a date two weeks from today's date.

Each morning, you look in your electronic calendar device for (or, your assistant places on your desk) those items you requested to review on that particular date. The idea is to keep issues from falling through the cracks and being forgotten. Also, if people in the organization get accustomed to hearing from you on the date that they agreed to fulfill an action request, they will take those commitments seriously.

Lastly, one of the best time management tools Rick had found comes from Stephen Covey's renowned book, *The Seven Habits of Highly Successful People*. Covey calls it the Time Management Matrix. This two-by-two square matrix is divided into quadrants. The quadrants are labeled *Urgent* and *Not Urgent* across the top; and *Important* and *Not Important* down the left side. The upper left quadrant is, therefore, a square labeled *Urgent* and *Important*. If, in reviewing the issues and decisions before you, you find one that meets the test of being both urgent and important, it belongs in this upper left Quadrant I. As an example, if it is April 15 and the item with which you are dealing is filing your income tax, it probably qualifies as a candidate for Quadrant I.

Quadrant I includes everything that is an immediate problem or crisis. It includes things which have a deadline of today. The idea is to minimize those issues which end up in this quadrant. Leaving deadlines or decisions to be accomplished when they reach crisis proportions is counterproductive and leads to poor results more often than not. By reviewing everything we are working on against this matrix, we strive to make assignments of the issues, initiatives, challenges, decisions, and actions with which we are confronted to one of the *other* quadrants.

The items assigned to Quadrant II are *important*, but *not urgent*. These will end up *being* urgent if we do not deal with them while they are still in this quadrant. Prevent crises by working in Quadrant II. In this quadrant, according to Covey, we plan, prepare, think critically, and seize opportunities. By working daily on the issues in Quadrant II, we minimize those which eventually make their way to Quadrant I. We work in Quadrant II to avoid being forced to work in crisis mode in Quadrant I.

Items which are listed in Quadrant III appear urgent, but are *not important*. The challenge for all of us as leaders is to avoid the mistake of wasting time on apparently urgent, but unimportant things — being, again, in the thick of thin things. Interrupting Quadrant I or II work to answer a ringing telephone is more than likely a distraction from an important task. The ringing phone seems urgent to us, and is usually not of immediate import.

Constantly checking the email inbox is also working in Quadrant III most of the time. Better to have your assistant screen email messages and send on to you only those he or she deems important. Your assistant should have authority to forward email to the person deemed most capable of or responsible for dealing with the issue.

Dropping everything to read "snail mail" is usually working in Quadrant III. It may *seem* urgent and important, but it is neither for the most part. And if your assistant believes something in the mail is important, he or she can alert you when you have finished the task at hand.

People will also try to influence you to deal with an issue which they believe to be urgent and important to *them*. Frequently, these items are neither in relation to the "big picture." Again, your assistant is your primary asset in your ability to maintain focus on Quadrant II, and occasionally Quadrant I. The issues of others may or may not be both urgent and important. A good assistant can usually sort these out effectively.

Quadrant IV contains things that are not urgent and not important — trivial things, busywork, pleasant activities designed to pass the time. They have no place in the work environment. They creep into the work place regularly, however. An example is the office March Madness pool. What could be more enjoyable than to while away the afternoon discussing selections for the NCAA basketball brackets?

Every office needs some frivolity. Rick's thought was to emphasize use of the Time Management Matrix with members of the organization; and, then leave them to their own good judgment. Raising everyone's conscientiousness regarding your thoughts on Quadrant IV is usually enough.

Black Rock State College had a good public relations (PR) director. She knew her business, was intimately familiar with the institution, and was an effective leader of her group of two other professionals and three support personnel. She was sensitive about the morale of her squad, which frequently worked long and odd hours; and, with some regularity, took them to a long lunch or other such team building diversion. Rick thought that she did this a little too often; but, her group was effective and he did not like to tamper with success.

Then one day while she and her group were off campus on one of these junkets, an incident occurred that required careful and immediate interaction with the media. Rick assembled the CLT to discuss their response to some fast-breaking developments. They agreed upon an approach; and Rick asked Bob Carlisle who was responsible for the PR area to call in the director so they could take advantage of her thinking. Bob soon informed him that the *entire* PR office was off campus. It was 2:30 PM.

After the PR staff returned from their extended lunch, Rick asked the director and Bob to join him in his office. Rick told the director that the college needed a minimum of one PR professional on campus at all times during normal business hours; and, that he thought that taking the *entire* group off campus during those hours was bad judgment. He also told her that she was a vital cog in the well-oiled machinery of the college and that he depended heavily on her opinion in matters involving the media. Rick indicated to the director that he thought she had let him and the college down at a critical moment; and, that this could not happen again. He also pointed out that he thought the group was playing too long in Quadrant IV. This he knew was understood, as they had discussed the Time Management Matrix together in the leadership development seminars.

Negative feedback is best delivered immediately upon experiencing a problem that requires redress. The director in this case was a responsible leader. She felt badly about the incident. They never had this problem again and Rick was careful to give her plenty of positive feedback when the occasion arose after this encounter. She became a better leader and more effective than ever.

This was a teachable moment for the public relations group. The nudge Rick gave the director helped them all to refocus on Quadrant I (where the incident placed them for a short time) and Quadrant II.

Rick frequently asked the question in CLT meetings when a new issue arose as to whether it was a Quadrant I or Quadrant II topic. This helped to keep them all focused on important issues, and avoided the tendency to "chase rabbits."

One of the criticisms that a few mal-content faculty had attempted to lay at Rick's doorstep was the inability to make decisions. This elicited a good bit of humorous conversation at meetings of the CLT.

The first axiom of effective decision-making is *not* to make important decisions until you have to. Some leaders (and some detractors) believe that it is important to make decisions quickly and often. The hubris of this fallacy is a problem in many organizations. Some leaders seem to pride themselves on their ability to decide expeditiously on a course of action, just because they have decision-making authority. They then move on to the next decision and do the same thing again. They *create* a Quadrant I mentality for decision-making, even though the urgency of the issue may be questionable.

What is *important* is to make the best decision possible in a timely manner, i.e. in Quadrant II. The first step in assessing alternatives is to determine at what future point in time the decision must be made — the point that it will move from Quadrant II to Quadrant I. Once this is determined, collect as much information as possible about alternative courses of action.

Some decisions are tied to other events. In other words, the timing (or even necessity) of some decisions may depend on a certain event (or chain of events) taking place. If these events do not take place, or are delayed, the original decision may not be as urgent or as important.

The more time that is available for decision-making, the more time there is to collect pertinent information and the more information there is that will become available. Also, more events will occur that may impact the choice. The more information we have, the better decision we can make.

The longer we can delay a strategic decision, the more *projected* events prove themselves to be real or not. Sometimes circumstances change so much that the original decision is not only not needed, it's options may prove to be ridiculous!

Don't fall prey to those who would accuse you of the inability to make decisions. The job of the CEO is to decide *when* to make a decision and what information is required prior to that time in order to act based upon facts, not emotion. Remember that the decision *not* to make a decision is also making a decision!

Decisions in organizations are too frequently based on emotion. This is an easy trap into which to fall. It is seductive to contemplate the popular decision based upon the emotion of the moment. It is essential to avoid this pitfall and to base decisions on well-founded facts about the situation.

Gathering accurate and relevant information is paramount. Most colleges and universities have researchers whose job it is to collect and analyze information about the organization's performance, environment and competitors. Without such a skill in the organization, you are doomed to less than optimum decisions.

Information is data endowed with meaning and relevance. Successful organizations have someone who is responsible for converting data into useful form. "Useful form" means that the information is accurate, relevant, impactful and easily understood. Easy to say, harder to accomplish.

Black Rock State College had such a person. She had her fingers on every piece of information Rick ever needed or wanted. He would have been lost without her. He frequently wondered if she realized how essential she was to the successes he enjoyed during his presidency. He resolved to make certain that he let her know!

Even though Rick had this wonderful organizational researcher collecting the relevant data he needed, he frequently found himself massaging what she gave him into a format that he believed helped to make it more easily understood and more impactful. Rick believed in the old adage, *"Liars figure, figures don't lie!"* He always wanted to present information for decision-making in the most dramatic and easily understood fashion.

Rick thought carefully before deciding on a way to present information to a constituency. It is important to assess the context for both the group receiving the information and for the data itself. How much can you expect the group to know about the topic? What helped *you* learn about the issue and understand it better? What visual aids (charts, graphs, trend lines, pictures, etc.) would assist people in developing insight?

Rick always analyzed information carefully with the CLT as an essential portion of decision-making. Everyone in the group saw the information in a different light — the light that illuminated *their* division of the college. Striving for consensus was the goal. Consensus was not always possible; but, the process of trying to reach it led to better decisions and a stronger team dynamic.

Once everyone involved clearly understood the context and environment surrounding an impending decision, had collected and studied the relevant information and facts, had weighed the options for action and had waited as long as possible for affiliated events to transpire; it was time to decide. Rick was always pleasantly surprised at how easy decision-making became with this approach!

During the course of his fourth year at BRSC, Rick and Bob Carlisle convinced alumnus Bill McElhenney, the home improvement mogul, to attend a NASCAR race with them and to meet Junior Samples. McElhenney had never been to a race before, let alone followed the sport. Junior had decided to try to purchase his own race team. When working as the driver for someone else, he split winnings on a 50-50 basis with the team owner. He was earning well over $1 million per year in this fashion. If he owned his own team, he could manage all the proceeds himself.

Bob Carlisle and Rick convinced Bill McElenney to accompany them to a race. Bill told them to go ahead and make the arrangements with Junior for the race track in Brooklyn, Michigan. He said that he would make the travel plans and for them to meet him at Dekalb-Peachtree Airport in Atlanta on the Friday afternoon before the race. They assumed from this that they would be guests on a flight to Michigan aboard Bill's corporate plane.

Bob, his wife Valerie, Sally and Rick arrived at Peachtree-Dekalb Airport before Bill and his wife. The pilot of the plane was there and he helped them to load their luggage and board. They awaited the McElhenneys.

The plane was a Gulfstream G-5, the pilot explained. That didn't mean much to Rick, but he could easily tell that it was special. It had large captain's chair seats bound in luxurious beige leather. These were all on swivels so they could face any direction. In between each two were polished mahogany tables which folded neatly into the fuselage of the plane. The floor was cherry hardwood. The ceiling and bulkheads were smoked mirrors. There was a TV monitor at each end of the cabin with a display of the plane's location on a map, its air speed, elevation and the estimated time of arrival at its destination.

The cabin windows were much larger than those on a commercial airliner. There were two large built-in polished mahogany coolers toward the rear. These were stocked with food and drink. In the rear was a lavatory.

Bill and his wife Janine arrived in short order. After they were settled, the plane began to taxi out to the runway for take-off. Rick remarked, "I've been on a number of corporate jets, Bill, but nothing a lovely as this one!"

"Rick, this isn't a corporate jet. This is *my* jet." Bill responded.

At that moment Rick realized that they were in the presence of *real* wealth!

"Guess what the deciding factor was regarding the purchase of *this* particular plane." Bill smiled.

"I dunno! Maybe the windows?" Rick guessed.

"Precisely!" laughed his host.

Bill McElhenney was taken with the spectacle of NASCAR Winston Cup racing. He could see how sponsorship of a race team could render publicity for the McElhenney brand. He and Junior discussed their mutual interests at the race in Michigan. Several weeks later, Bill decided to take race team sponsorship to the McElhenney board of directors. After a presentation by Junior, who was a superior spokesperson, the McElhenney board concluded that the company would sign a contract with him to sponsor his race team for two years with the option to sign for two more, assuming things worked out as planned.

Junior Samples and Bill McElhenney were elated at their partnership. Junior was beholding to BRSC for bringing the two of them together and making it possible for him to purchase the race team. After that, he couldn't do enough for the college with regard to bringing alumni to races and feting them behind the scenes where they could meet the drivers, attend driver meetings and watch the race from Junior's pit. Relationship building with influential and well-heeled alumni was going swimmingly!

Chapter Nine

Reorganizing to Accommodate Fiscal Reality

"To avoid criticism, say nothing, do nothing, be nothing." —Robert Gates

Rick was nothing if not cognizant of the ill will and stress generated by downsizing the workforce to accommodate budget reality. Institutional budgets beget more skepticism and distrust than any other aspect of college life. Some members of the organization always seem to believe that the administration has ways to horde precious resources. Indeed, this may be the case. Leaders need to have contingency monies on hand for the unforeseen circumstances that always arise.

The best way to put the minds of skeptics to rest and to minimize expenditure of wasted energy and distraction searching for these funds is to divulge them to the campus. Rick decided on full disclosure for the entire budget — total revenue generated by tuition, fees, room, board, state tax allocations, federal and state grants, research grants, unrestricted and restricted donations, federal and state need-based financial aid, and other money flowing from entrepreneurial endeavors; and expenditures for salaries, fringe benefits, supplies, equipment, utilities, etc. — to the campus community. This was done in a simplified manner, as budget management/accounting jargon risks misunderstanding.

Here is what Rick did at BRSC. The department heads and directors estimated operating expenses for the upcoming year. These included the cost of salaries and fringe benefits for faculty and staff, supplies, equipment, consumables, and overhead — the cost of space utilization, telephone, reproduction, wireless network, etc. The costs for laboratory intensive programs exceeded those for their non-lab counterparts, but the goal was for these costs to be less than revenue generated by student enrollment plus research grants;

otherwise some aspects of departmental operations were candidates for cost reduction. Like any other, the higher education enterprise needed a positive cash flow to survive. This approach utilized a zero-based budget process, not just a spin-off of last year's numbers.

When every department, academic and non-academic, had prepared a budget request using the same format, the information was shared across the campus in summary form so that each department understood the total resources being requested institution-wide. It was thus obvious when total funds requested exceeded total revenue generated. Then, negotiations commenced to determine how *available* resources would be allocated.

Rick made certain that department leaders were all using the same template for preparation of annual budget requests. The BRSC comptroller determined the actual cost to operate each academic program and department. The comptroller then determined the tuition that was generated by the student-credit hours (SCH) produced by each department. The total revenue generated by a department was then compared with the total cost to operate the department. If the revenue did not exceed the cost, low enrollment academic programs might be upgraded to increase enrollment, or considered for elimination, if that was not possible.

Once budgets for each department were finalized, the institution-wide budget, again in summary form, was shared with the entire campus. There was no need to expose salaries, just totals by department. This dispelled rumors and innuendo that the administration was hoarding precious resources. It also exposed administrative overhead for all to view.

Rick held in reserve for contingency purposes the unused portions of salaries and fringe benefits of people who retired, resigned, or otherwise left the organization during the course of a fiscal year. There was usually a gap between such attrition and the time when the position was filled again. This supported a fairly significant contingency fund — about $150,000 per year (at this writing) for every 100 employees on the payroll.

The goal was to demystify the budget and its allocation process as much as possible. Time and energy spent to this end was worth the peace of mind it created across the campus.

Twenty-first century leadership of colleges and universities requires constant attention to costs and ways to reduce them. Global competition has made controlling costs essential in the corporate realm for years. Scarce resources produce the same pressure in the government and not-for-profit sectors, as well.

Cost analysis is easier than it was 15 or 20 years ago due to electronic information gathering tools increasingly available. Leaders should monitor developments that bring new technology to bear on their operational processes and assist in reducing costs. Most institutions have a CIO (chief information officer) to help with this initiative.

Evolving technology also renders existing business practices and activities obsolete or nonessential quickly these days. One of the goals at BRSC was to strive to eliminate as many unnecessary activities as possible. People become accustomed to and comfortable with a well understood and reasonably effective modus operandi. Rick and the CLT searched for ways to encourage members of the organization to consider new more effective and efficient methods. This was not an easy proposition. If they came right out and suggested that they believed people in the business operations of the college were not functioning as efficiently and effectively as they might, the CLT ran the risk of alienating them or, worse, leaving them with the impression that the CLT thought that it knew better than the employees did how to do their jobs. It doesn't matter how much experience you may have, it would be surprising if you knew more about operational details than the people actually performing the functions.

Here are a couple of suggestions designed to zero in on methods of operation, functional efficiency and effectiveness, and productivity. These helped the college to visualize how work was accomplished and the appropriate resources required to perform specific functions.

A key was finding an innocuous way to encourage people to investigate on their own their ways of doing business. Rick and the CLT asked them to make flow diagrams of their operational processes so that the CLT might begin to learn how they function. These process flow diagrams were more appropriate for the business functions of BRSC than they were for classroom activities. They included each activity that comprised the function of the particular team or department.

Rick believed that this technique was applicable to the offices of admissions, financial aid, registrar and academic record keeping, food service, accounting, procurement, accounts payable, accounts receivable, institutional advancement, physical plant, career planning/placement, health center, public safety, mail service, telephone service, information technology, human resources/benefits, and the like. The National Science Foundation document NSF-67-15 entitled, *Systems for Measuring and Reporting the Resources and Activities of Colleges and Universities* is an excellent resource, even 45 years after its publication.

Process flow diagrams are standard tools in organizations involved in manufacturing, production, or construction. They are also useful to colleges and universities. So states the book, *Productivity and Higher Education*, edited by Richard E. Anderson and Joel W. Meyerson. These authors suggest *macro* flow diagram analysis. Rick preferred micro analysis; here's why.

The purpose of preparing process flow diagrams is to provide members of a department or team with an opportunity to think critically about their functions and how they perform them. Those actually doing the work are in the best position to analyze it and to make recommendations to improve it. Once the work flow is described in picture form, employees and/or leaders may recognize steps that are unnecessary, redundant, or incorrect based on organizational policies, customer desires or current technology.

At BRSC, they assembled process flow diagrams from almost every facet of institutional operations, with the exception of teaching. These were then shared across the institution so employees began to garner an appreciation for one another's functions. Leaders also had an opportunity to learn more about these processes and perhaps question the "whys and wherefores" of some operating procedures.

In the end, the goal was to have in place an approach which allowed for continuous review and analysis of the way in which the organization conducted its business. This, in turn, provided an opportunity to continuously improve basic operations, leading to more efficient and effective processes and a more competitive posture in the market place.

Employees at BRSC needed reassurance during these proceedings that their jobs were not at stake — indeed, that the college was not asking them to investigate eliminating portions of their work in order to reduce the size of the work force. The goal was to eliminate *unnecessary* work, so that people were available to perform other (and often new) functions. In the long view, the goal was to reduce the size of the work force through natural attrition as people resigned or retired, not through lay-offs.

Process flow diagrams should be updated at least once every two years, if not annually. This should become part of departmental unit/team strategic planning. Employee evaluation should be tied to departmental improvement, as well as individual accomplishments. More details regarding preparation of process flow diagrams are provided in Appendix IV.

Unit productivity factors are another cost control/reduction tool. This approach may smack of Frederick Taylor-style scientific work method analysis which permeated the early 20th century industrial revolution and mass production techniques. Unit productivity factors are, however, applicable in almost *every* work setting; and, can provide valuable insight into trends in organizational efficiency and effectiveness at colleges and universities. If the term *unit productivity factor* offends, change it to *assessment factor.*

College and university leaders need to balance finite or decreasing fiscal resources with expanding enrollment and activities. This usually means that the institution must constantly search for ways to become more efficient and effective. Personnel costs (salaries and fringe benefits) are 70% or more of the total budget for knowledge-based organizations like those in academia or hospitals or symphony orchestras.

Productivity is the ratio of inputs to outputs. It improves when an increase in output occurs per unit of input. The goal is to enhance efficiency and effectiveness within fiscal constraints.

It is hard to imagine a product or service that does not, in some way, result in measurable parameters. If there are three employees working with the university's customers to receive tuition and fee payments and they handle a total of 300 transactions in a daily shift, then each teller averages 100 of these transactions per work shift. Longitudinal data should be available for past years regarding the number of transactions and employees working them at various times of the day/week/month/year. It should be relatively easy to plot a trend line of the average number of transactions per employee per day or per hour for the last few years. Five years of historical data should be sufficient, since payment technology changes significantly in that time.

The number of transactions per teller per unit of time (year, month, week, day, or hour) is called a unit (one employee per hour, say) productivity/assessment factor. In this example, it was determined that an employee can handle about 100 transactions per work day, or about 17 per hour, assuming a six hour shift at the payment window.

This type of information helps the university decide on appropriate staffing levels and whether overall efficiency is trending up or down. If productivity is trending downward, these data will flag the condition for review by the department head or leadership team.

The US Government Bureau of Labor Statistics (www.bls.gov) has gathered, analyzed and published unit productivity information for various types of businesses and industries over the last several decades. This information is available and useful to those engaged in similar working environments. Colleges and universities may need to create their own databases. The Integrated Postsecondary Education Data System (IPEDS) has relevant data, as well (www.nces.ed.gov/ipeds).

Assessing faculty productivity was one of the most controversial conversations on the BRSC campus. Teaching *productivity* (as opposed to *effectiveness*) was fairly easy to quantify. The best assessment factor for teaching productivity was the number of student-credit-hours generated per faculty member per semester. This was calculated by multiplying the number of students in each class taught by a given faculty member by the credit-hour value of that class. The student-credit-hours per class were accumulated for all the classes taught by this faculty member for the semester. The experience at BRSC was that 250-275 student-credit-hours (SCH) per faculty member per semester was appropriate for coursework involving a laboratory experience; and 350-400 SCH for non-lab coursework. These parameters are applicable for a primarily undergraduate institution.

The teaching factors were useful in determining the appropriate number of faculty required by each department at BRSC. If the department teaches non-laboratory coursework and the total number of student-credit-hours generated by the department is 3,500 for the semester, then using a factor of 350 SCH/faculty member results in the need for 10 faculty positions. The book,

Managing Faculty Resources by G. Gregory Lozier and Michael J. Dooris suggests using "position control" at some higher school/college/institutional/system level to reallocate vacant faculty positions between disciplines.

At BRSC, they averaged the SCH factor over a department, rather than expecting that every faculty member would carry the appropriate load. This gave the department head flexibility in assigning teaching load. If someone received a lighter teaching load (in terms of SCHs) in a given semester, this could be rotated to a different faculty member in the next semester and overall SCH factor departmental goals could still be realized.

Other useful faculty productivity/assessment factors are research grant dollars generated per faculty member per year by department; and cost per credit hour of delivery of education (divide the total instructional budget by the total number of credit hours undertaken by students for the given semester).

Almost *every* function in every type of organization (corporate, governmental, not-for-profit, manufacturing, service, construction, higher education, etc.) can be quantified with some type of unit productivity/assessment factor approach. Every organization should collect data and calculate factors that illuminate efficiency and effectiveness. Even if this has never been done before, it is relatively easy to do with the use of longitudinal data from the last several years of operation. If these types of data do not exist, start determining what they should be and begin to collect them. Then, start watching trends. Some examples of the types of data that were collected at BRSC are included in the Appendix V.

The unit productivity/assessment factor approach supports planning and decision making based on facts and relevant information. The likelihood of making good decisions when basing actions on facts is enhanced. When the University System HQ, the chancellor or the Board of Regents questioned decisions, it helped Rick to have factual details at his fingertips to support actions.

The BRSC CLT decided early on that as part of supporting a thrust to increase enrollment, they should provide a wireless environment for students as a part of long range strategic planning. At the end of Rick's fourth year, the college realized the wireless campus strategic goal and Yahoo designated BRSC as the third most wired campus in the nation. This was an incredible accomplishment for a small public institution in a remote location. The college made a lot of marketing hay with that recognition!

Chapter Ten

You Have to Love It When the Plan Comes Together

"Leadership is the art of getting someone else to do something you want done because he wants to do it." —Dwight D. Eisenhower

The Strategic Plan, which was now operationalized throughout the BRSC campus, led to a pipeline of new academic programs of study under development and coming to fruition. These were attractive to potential students and employers of graduates and resulted in steadily increasing enrollment. Enhanced enrollment led, in turn, to additional funding from state allocations and increased revenue generation from tuition and fees, residence hall room rental, food service operations and other concessions.

At this point, four years into his administration, Rick had finally assembled an experienced and effective cadre of officers to carry out day-to-day operation of the institution. That freed him to focus more on relationship building and fundraising. Bob Carlisle and he were able to secure the college's largest gift to date — $500,000 in support of an academic program from which the donor had graduated.

Action was being taken by individual faculty and staff members according to their assignments from the Strategic Plan. At year end, every employee received a performance evaluation. Everyone in a working organization should receive an evaluation at least once per year. This seems a statement of the obvious, but all too often it does not occur.

Entry level people at BRSC underwent an evaluation every six months for their first two years. Evaluations were onerous, arduous, and sometimes unpleasant. They were also essential to creating a team of enthusiastic, motivated people. And, they were crucial for those occasions where the college needed to ask someone to look elsewhere for employment.

Most of us want and need feedback regarding our contribution. We want insight as to how we are performing in the eyes of those who have input into how much money we make, how quickly we can expect to move up in the organizational hierarchy, and how we can improve our performance. Most of us are receptive to constructive feedback designed to help us enhance our value to the organization.

Some will suggest that evaluation of tenured, senior faculty is inappropriate. Horse hockey! Everyone needs to know what the institution expects of them and how they are doing. Every self-respecting organization has a formal annual evaluation process at every level of employment so members receive feedback regarding performance *prior* to learning about annual salary adjustments. Organizations that do not do this are functioning below their potential. This process should be conducted over a period of weeks immediately *prior* to decisions and announcements regarding compensation adjustments and/or promotion.

Shortly after he became department chair at Grable State, Rick had a challenging time sorting out when to be a strong faculty advocate, and when to be a strong leader in the college administration. There was no written description of his duties. Early on, he erred on the side of the faculty — an error which *they* loved! His boss the dean, however, did not love it!

Instead of calling Rick in for eyeball to eyeball feedback, his boss sent him a terse letter providing a good deal of negative feedback and indicating a poor salary adjustment for the year in question. Rick received this letter on a Friday. He immediately called his boss to see if he could arrange a meeting to discuss the situation. Rick was informed that the dean was not on campus. He was forced to wait until Monday to meet — a planned "cooling off period," no doubt.

Well, that's one approach. It lacks courage, though. This boss and Rick grew to become great friends and collaborators, primarily because the dean was a believer in second chances. Without second chances, many of us would be sunk!

Here is a better approach. A vital part of any evaluation process is the existence of job descriptions for every function in the organization. Job descriptions provide an outline of organizational responsibilities. These descriptions tell employees what is expected of them. Job descriptions should be written by the supervisor for the position with input from the employees actually performing the functions. Job descriptions deal with the contributions that people are expected to make and the responsibilities they are expected to accept in the work setting. Some examples are provided in Appendix VI.

Employees in leadership positions should undergo a "360 degree evaluation." This involves asking the employee's supervisor, peers, and direct reports to evaluate her or him utilizing a standard evaluation instrument such as that suggested in Appendix VI. The *quantitative* responses to the evaluation should be averaged over the group performing the evaluation, or by like evaluator (peers, direct reports, etc.). Written *qualitative* feedback should be presented anonymously. The employee and the supervisor should receive the quantitative averages and the written feedback *after* it has been summarized confidentially by a third party, usually the Human Resources Department.

The immediate supervisor should then meet with the employee being evaluated to review feedback and to establish a plan for performance for the next year. This is also the appropriate time for salary adjustment conversations.

An effective performance evaluation process improves employee contributions and attitude. It also creates a history and provides continuity for a new supervisor to rely upon; and, for those occasions when someone is asked to leave the institution.

After vision and mission statements have been prepared, institutional goals and objectives have been developed, job descriptions have been written, and individual performance reviews have been conducted, it is important to recognize and reward achievement. If goals and objectives have quantifiable date-certain outcome measures, it is easy to assess achievements. The identity of those members of the organization responsible for successes should also be easy to determine. Assigning appropriate rewards can be more challenging.

If the college or university is a private one with no union or state budget constraint with which to deal, the flexibility may exist to award salary increases and bonuses as conditions warrant. In public institutions and/or when collective bargaining agreements are in place, this may be more challenging. Nonetheless, money speaks volumes to most folks; and a permanent salary increase is usually better than a onetime bonus.

Salary increases may be constrained for public institutions by state, county, or municipal guidelines. Many times, if one individual is awarded a relatively large salary increase, another (or, several others) will necessarily receive lesser adjustments so that the overall salary increase allocation will not be exceeded.

Most institutions will have discretionary or non-state funds (usually resulting from unrestricted external donations or revenue generation) which may be utilized for one time awards to recognize substantial contributions. This allows the flexibility to provide some bonuses commensurate with individual achievements and contributions.

When salary adjustments and bonuses have been awarded to the extent possible, there are other means of recognition that are effective. If members of the organization believe that they are being compensated fairly with respect to their peers and their profession in general, most will understand the constraints under which academic institutions operate.

Colleges and universities usually have several gatherings of faculty and staff each academic year. Black Rock State hosted New Student Convocation for incoming freshmen each fall, presidential "state-of-the-college" remarks for faculty and staff at the beginning of each semester, Honors Convocation in late spring, Commencement at the end of the academic year, and after that a service awards luncheon for all employees. All of these ceremonies provided a forum for public recognition of worthy contributions. Such recognition was accomplished by presenting organizational members with an engraved silver platter, a personalized college rocking or captain's chair, or the like. If significant monetary reward is not an option, this type of recognition goes a long way towards demonstrating appreciation for a job well done.

It is worth noting that *continuous* recognition of "little kindnesses" or exemplary customer service is appropriate. The Director of Human Resources at BRSC instituted a peer recognition program whereby any member of the organization could nominate another for special recognition regarding the well-being of the college and its clientele.

The idea here was for people who observed their peers making some kind of special contribution to suggest that they receive recognition. At BRSC, this ranged from a campus police officer assisting students (and parents) on fall semester "move-in" day by helping to carry belongings into residence halls, to a faculty member driving commuter students home when they had missed their car pool, to volunteering to keep score at athletic events, to being an especially effective advisor to a student organization. A peer review committee met once per semester to judge the nominations.

Each public gathering provided an opportunity to honor and celebrate the successes of the institution and its members. It also helped the college to keep track of progress. At the end of every academic year, Rick issued a communiqué to the campus listing achievements for the year. It always amazed him that the college had accomplished so much, even though day-to-day progress seemed incredibly slow.

People are perhaps the only organizational asset that *appreciates* over time. Facilities, supplies and equipment *depreciate* with time. After identifying, recruiting, hiring, and retaining excellent people, the next most important task is to develop them so that they may realize their aspirations and full potential in the organization.

The CLT and Rick spent a good deal of time defining the characteristics that ought to be present in an "excellent employee." People who are the most effective employees manage themselves well. They are well organized and budget their time efficiently — they have learned to work primarily in Quadrant II of Covey's Time-Management Matrix. They are able to work independently with minimal supervision. They are resourceful and leaders are comfortable delegating responsibility to them. These employees understand the goals and objectives of the organization, and are committed to working towards them.

Effective employees are focused on higher performance standards than the work environment requires. Life-long learning is second nature to them. They continuously master skills useful to the institution and to their own careers. These folks view co-workers as colleagues, not competitors; and they contribute well in teams.

Excellent people earn the trust and respect of their co-workers. They give credit where credit is due. These folks also stand up for their values and beliefs. One of the major jobs of supervisors is to find, hire and retain people with these qualities.

Most people are interested in maximizing their value to the organization. Part of the annual performance review process should be establishment of a plan for professional growth for *each member* of the institution. This might include provisions for people to: 1) earn additional educational credentials; 2) attend appropriate professional meetings and conferences; 3) participate in professional development short courses; and 4) work in a new or different job to learn new skills valued by the organization.

The professional development plan for each individual should also list personal career aspirations, complete with appropriate building blocks for achieving these goals. Building blocks may include advanced degrees and/or a series of different job assignments providing preparation for advancement. This process will alert organizational members that the institution is interested in their growth and development and plans for the future. It also helps the college or university plan a "succession tree" of people who will step into various roles of ever-increasing responsibility as the need arises or the opportunity presents itself. Every leader should have as a task the development of someone to take his or her place in the organization. People are continuously retiring, resigning, or being promoted. The institution needs to know who will take over when these circumstances arise. And, it's usually less risky to "grow your own" from within, rather than to hire from outside.

There was a steep hill behind the BRSC campus that led up to Black Rock Mountain State Park. It was lovely up there what with virgin forests, a population of deer, turkey and red fox, to say nothing of the flocks of birds and squads of squirrels. Rick was disturbed to learn that groups of students were congregating high up for what they called "hill parties" on Wednesday nights. Hill parties amounted to upper class students who were 21 years or older purchasing kegs of beer and then selling 16 ounce plastic cups to under aged students for $10 for all they could drink. To make matters worse, apparently the under aged folks, in an attempt to achieve a buzz in a hurry, were using funnels with which to pour beer from their cups down their throats! Faculty were noticing a high rate of absenteeism on Thursday mornings.

Rick was appalled to learn about these gatherings and directed that the university police raid them, check identification and confiscate the kegs and tapping apparatus, if it was concluded that under aged students were being served. The police suggested that this policy would merely drive students off campus to drink and that they would then need to drive back. So, there was the concern about driving under the influence. Rick and Dave Bradford decided that they just couldn't tolerate allowing the hill parties to continue on college property with their knowledge.

"Let's you and I go along with the police on one of their raids to eyeball this for ourselves!" Rick suggested. So up they went about midnight on a Wednesday.

As they climbed in the dark, the two (along with their escort of university police) came upon a small bonfire in a clearing. Standing around it in a large group were about 30 students. As they came closer, one of the students yelled out, "Who's the old f---er coming up the hill?"

Since Rick was leading the group, he assumed this comment was directed his way.

"I'll tell you who it is!" he yelled back. There was an immediate exodus in all directions from the area! All that remained was the keg and the tap which the officers confiscated.

Rick asked the faculty to mention in their classes that hill parties were discontinued and that anyone caught in similar circumstances would be asked to continue their studies at a different institution of higher learning. The police continued their patrols and the issue went away. Rick had forgotten all about it by the time commencement rolled around that May. As one of the graduating seniors came across the stage, receiving his diploma and stopping to shake hands with Rick (as they all did), he said, "May I please have my tap back now?"

Rick erupted into laughter! He hadn't been certain that students realized exactly who raided their party those months ago. He was glad that he was recognized and remembered, to say nothing of this particular student's sense of humor. It always helps to have a good memory!

Chapter Eleven

Rules of the Road

"By the time it had come to the edge of the forest the stream had grown up, so that it was almost a river, and being grown up, it did not run and jump and sparkle along as it used to do when it was younger, but moved more slowly. For it now knew where it was going, and it said to itself, 'There is no hurry, we shall get there some day.'" —A. A. Milne from *Winnie-the-Pooh*

Rick had some philosophical ideas and approaches that helped him earn the organizational trust and respect that is essential for success as a leader. First, he tried to avoid creating expectations that could not be fulfilled. He was cautious about making promises. He made them only when he was positive that he could deliver. Broken promises and unmet expectations undermine leadership.

Late in his tenure as head of the Psychology Department at Grable State, Rick's boss, the dean, expressed to him at year end that Rick had done a good job; but, that he was only able to offer a minimal increase in salary, due to budget constraints. Rick asked if the dean thought he could count on a commensurately larger raise the next year to compensate for the current small one. The dean responded with positive enthusiasm and said that he would pursue that. He was no doubt glad to get off the hook for the time being.

The next year, it was "déjà vu all over again." Rick never heard a word about a larger raise. He believed that he should have made an issue of it; but, was so disheartened that he could not bring himself to initiate a conversation about it with his boss.

If you are promised an increase in salary and one is not forthcoming, your trust is seriously eroded. Likewise, if politicians promise improvements in health care, education, energy independence, or the economy and none result, we begin to lose confidence in them; or, we should. It was Rick's boss's responsibility to represent him in salary conversations with *his* boss, and he had let Rick down. It took a couple of years for Rick to trust the dean again.

Secondly, Rick made it a point to *apologize* when he was wrong. Some believe that they should never apologize or admit that they were wrong. How silly! Think how absurd we look trying to cover our posteriors, to say nothing of trying to argue for a failed plan. Instead, why not take full responsibility and apologize. Rick would also indicate how much he had learned from the experience and how much better he would be able to perform in the future as a result. When he as leader took responsibility, he allowed the rest of the organization off the hook. That enabled everyone to get back to work without expending wasted energy on the blame game, and worrying about their own posteriors. The larger the responsibility, the bigger the mistakes and their impact. As president, Rick made some whoppers! These were burdensome and distracting, so he resolved to adjust his approach and start again, putting them behind him as soon as possible. Because people in the BRSC organization trusted and respected Rick, they allowed him to do this.

Thirdly, Rick tried not to *surprise* members of the organization with bad or controversial news. He let them know that *he* did not like surprises, either. It is *never* better to withhold unpleasant news. Rick tried to let people know in a timely manner what to expect. He told them what he was dealing with, and how he planned to handle it. People are, for the most part, mature enough to adjust to change, even change for the worse, if they understand the circumstances and have *time* to adjust to it. None of us are good at dealing with instantaneous upheaval. Besides, by sharing difficult challenges, members of the organization had a chance to participate in the resolution. Many had ideas worthy of consideration. Rick detested being caught short with a surprise — unless, of course, it was good news. We are all better served as leaders by insisting that we be informed of impending bad news as soon as possible. This gives us more time to respond intelligently. Of course, a leader can only expect to *receive* negative news, if he or she encourages this approach. Shooting the messenger will assure that we get no negative messages in the future. A calm and grateful response to information regarding gloomy potential events is always best.

Fourth, Rick kept no secrets. He shared information freely — the good, the bad, and the ugly. Members of the organization were more effective in their jobs when they were able to avail themselves of pertinent information. Uncertainty absorbs a great deal of institutional energy.

Fifth, Rick tried *never* to "get into a pissin' contest with a skunk." When he did, he learned quickly that he came away covered in stink. The corollary of this axiom is to always take the high road. As a leader, some will assume that you are fair game for rebuke for various reasons. If you are a public figure, you will, no doubt, experience a good deal of this; a corporate leader, perhaps less so. It *is* lonely at the top. Some, who do not have responsibility for positive outcomes, think they know better how to deal with the challenges facing the campus. The leader usually has more and better information than they do, so Rick didn't allow himself to get drawn into a contest between personalities. Legitimate debate is fine, indeed healthy, so long as *you* control the forum. Never raise your voice or lose your cool. Whatever the issue, it is usually not life threatening. Try to keep crisis in perspective. Your job is to de-escalate the situation.

Anyway, a key to this kind of potential abuse is the sixth point which is: "*never* let the sons-of-bitches see you sweat." Always strive to remain calm and outwardly unperturbed, no matter how outrageous the claims. Be gracious when others were being obnoxious. Professionalism generally unnerves the abuser; and magnanimity impresses constituents. Keeping cool under fire is an invaluable asset. Your staff will be more apt to follow your lead if they view you as having the strength to remain stable, unperturbed and solid when under stress.

Seventh, Rick avoided *any* type of duplicitous behavior. That meant laying his cards on the table with candor and forthrightness for all to see. If he was unable to persuade people of the value of his approach by emphatically stating his case, he knew that he probably had a poor case.

Eighth, and this is really a corollary to the seventh, Rick avoided criticizing others when they were not present to defend themselves. As Stephen Covey says, "Be loyal to those *not* in your presence, and you will (build great trust and respect) with those who *are* in your presence." When someone began to discuss with him the sins of someone not present, Rick would say something like, "Sounds like you feel strongly about this issue. Perhaps you should discuss it with (and name the person under discussion)." End of conversation! If we allow ourselves to be drawn into a conversation regarding the sins of others, what does our conversation partner learn about us? Why, that we will discuss *them* behind *their* back, given the opportunity. Few things erode trust more than talking about others when they are not present.

After he had been president of BRSC for several years, Rick failed to follow his own advice and let himself detour off the high road with the then president of the Faculty Senate. Rick made the colossal blunder (in an attempt to enhance meeting effectiveness) of telling him in front of the Senate executive committee that he thought the joint monthly meetings between him and his leadership team and Rick and the CLT were unproductive. What a sophomoric mistake!

This Faculty Senate president decided to initiate a survey of faculty and staff to assess support for Rick's administration. The survey had two parts. The first portion used a numerical scale to grade performance and perceptions of the leadership team. The second (and this was an unusually subtle move) asked for subjective responses to open ended questions — leading questions, at that! The numerically graded results showed solid support for and trust in Rick, the CLT and the college's agenda. The qualitative feedback, however, gave those with an agenda of their own (and there are always some) an opportunity to *really* unload. It was *not* pretty!

The Faculty Senate was comprised of representatives of all of the college's professional employees — about 275 faculty and staff. The negative feedback came from less than 10% of them. These comments were all anonymous, of course. The only critics that you should take seriously, incidentally, are those with the courage to identify themselves.

In the main, Rick was pleased and reassured by the feedback. The negative subjective comments were hurtful and stressful to read; but, were so unprofessional that he had an outpouring of support from those who were offended by the tone. The document was, of course, circulated throughout the campus. Rick's leadership team advised him to ignore the entire document, as it was positive in the main. He, however, decided that this was a teachable moment. He had a unique opportunity to demonstrate some of his leadership philosophy to both his immediate team and to the greater organization.

He set up a series of one hour appointments with all of the members of the Faculty Senate — about 40 people. Rick met individually with each of these folks over a period of about two months. He learned, as he had suspected going in, that he had the strong support of most. He also learned of some issues that he probably should have been on top of, but was not. The exercise was refreshing, professional, enlightening, and reassuring.

Shortly after concluding his dialogue with the Senators, Rick had an occasion to address all the members of the BRSC organization at the opening of fall semester. This was his opportunity, twice per year, to present the agenda for the semester, to discuss the financial well-being of the institution, to assess results against plans, and the like. At the end of these remarks, Rick said the following.

> *I apologize to those of you who found it necessary to get my attention with the recent survey. I take full responsibility for that outcome. I have spoken with all of the Faculty Senators over the summer about the feedback. I learned much from these conversations. I want you to know that I will always welcome your feedback, as long as it is conducted in a way that does not negatively impact the college's agenda or its clientele.*

After the presentation, a senior faculty member approached Rick and said, "Rick, your strength and influence as leader of Black Rock State will never be greater than they there are at this moment."

This reinforced Rick's opinion that he had successfully demonstrated humility and the ability to accept responsibility for the results he produced, to apologize when wrong, and to claim the high road. He came out of that episode in a stronger position than ever to lead Black Rock State. If served lemons, try to make lemonade.

Rick had also taught his leadership team a good lesson. Incidentally, *three* of them are now college presidents.

Chapter Twelve

The Centennial Celebration

"A centennial celebration is a wonderful excuse to raise money!"
—Rick Nedic

One of Black Rock State's most successful alumni was CEO of Georgia Peach Bank in Atlanta. Georgia Peach was the largest locally owned bank in the state. Harry Rex Thornton was also active in Republican politics. Rick had made a point of meeting with him shortly after arriving at the college. Harry Rex was proud of his affiliation with BRSC and that made him an easy sell for membership in the Black Rock State College President's Club. Membership cost $1,000 per year and included admission to all of the college's various athletic events and performing arts programs. It also included an invitation to the annual President's Club Banquet which gave Rick an opportunity to bring this vital group of supporters up to speed with the latest developments at the college and its most significant needs.

Newly elected Republican Governor Sonny Purdue was supportive of the excellent University System which he inherited. In fact, he was a has-been University of Georgia football athlete. He replaced Chancellor Mike Talbot with corporate CEO Lamar Hendricks who was looking for another challenge after a successful run leading a large Midwestern pharmaceutical firm. Rick looked forward with anticipation to working with Hendricks because he suspected the new chancellor would view the higher education enterprise more as a business with the constant need to assess results, minimize waste, reduce costs, improve performance and grow, all at the same time. That was the way Rick was attempting to operate at BRSC.

Rick was elated when, shortly after taking office, Gov. Purdue appointed Harry Rex to the University System Board of Regents. Imagine BRSC's good fortune! The college had an alum on the System governing body! Who could ask for more — Rick now had a concerned ear whenever he needed to run an idea up the flagpole or get an inside perspective on the direction of the System.

As the college attempted to build endowment and enhance fundraising initiatives, Rick and the CLT approached alumni, employers of graduates and vendors who sold supplies and materials to the campus. In academic year 2006-07, Rick's sixth, BRSC received almost $6 million is donations. Over half of this total was gifts-in-kind of laboratory equipment and consumables which helped the college introduce new programs and support existing ones without exceeding budget allocation. That year, *The Chronicle of Higher Education* named the college as having raised the seventh largest amount of money for undergraduate public colleges in the nation. Rick was exceptionally proud of that accomplishment.

The cable network MTV was a particular favorite with BRSC students. Dave Bradford, working with the Student Activities staff that reported to him, secured a video recording date for MTV at BRSC for the fall 2007. The TV network camped out on campus for three days, setting up several entertainment venues in one of the main parking lots. These mini film studios were mobbed by students during every break from classes, and sometimes during classes! The CLT and Rick joined in the fun and enjoyed being part of a national network production.

Rick believed that, in order to keep an organization aligned and moving as briskly as possible in the desired direction, it was important to teach techniques that helped to develop leaders at every level. These included some of the things discussed in this book — decision making, time management, meeting management, personnel evaluation, successful hiring techniques, a common (across departments) and open budget development process, strategic planning and implementation, sharing of information and the like.

To achieve this, Rick held weekly leadership sessions lasting one hour. The purpose of these gatherings was twofold. First, he wanted the leaders (department chairs, directors, deans, VPs, and faculty senate officers) in the organization to speak the same language regarding the areas mentioned above. If everyone at all levels of the organization expects meeting agendas to appear in the same format with outcome expectations and time limits, the organization will waste little time in unproductive gatherings. If everyone uses a common approach to budget preparation, everyone will be better able to understand one another's requests for funding, to say nothing of the decisions made as a result. When asked if an issue resides in Quadrant I or II, everyone understands the question and quickly makes an assignment to one of the time management matrix squares; and, more importantly, they understand immediately why we are not spending time and energy on issues in Quadrant III or IV.

Secondly, these sessions gave Rick an opportunity to present his leadership philosophy to the greater organization. "Leadership philosophy" was code for his expectations for *their* performance as leaders. Here, he wanted to impress upon them his desire that they would whole-heartedly buy into the organizational objectives and strategies that the college had developed and adopted. Rick wanted them to realize that once the strategic planning process was complete, the organization was going to be moving forward to implement the plans and achieve the goals; and, that the time for debate about these was finished.

A few leaders were more interested in keeping their positions of leadership and its benefits than in helping the organization to move forward. Identification of these folks was easier if they openly oppose organizational initiatives. This behavior usually manifested itself as the desire to debate issues already laid to rest, foot dragging with relation to assignments, and failure to meet deadlines. These overt responses are observable and may be addressed as they occur.

The subtle "passive resistant" leader is more difficult to discover. This is the leader who gives positive lip service to the organizational agenda, and then quietly and in private tells his or her people that "this too shall pass," and not to worry about it. We get no visible telltale of this type of behavior for a period of time, so it is more difficult to uncover. That is why quantifiable performance evaluation is worthwhile. Unless progress against organizational and individual goals and objectives is obvious when performance is assessed, it is time for serious counseling and/or a change in leadership for the area involved.

In a college or university setting the atmosphere is more conducive to ongoing debate. This renders some institutions resistant to change. It is the prerogative of organizational members in colleges and universities to debate the direction of the institution. It is *not*, however, the prerogative of anyone in a *leadership* position to do so. Rick wanted people at BRSC to understand that if they wanted to be a leader, they had better be able to support organizational goals and objectives. The hour-long leadership development sessions were designed to accomplish this.

Sally and the Rainbow Union were making progress and she was enjoying her role as "mother" and advisor to LGBT students. She worked with the chief information officer to establish a plan for protecting the identity of those who were not "out." This required posting a secure telephone number for students to call to obtain recorded information about meetings of the group and to leave messages. The IT department arranged for Sally to have sole access to this telephone number. She monitored it frequently and called those students who wished more confidential information. Crank calls to this number ceased after a couple of years and the group grew to include about 30 members. About two-thirds of these were gay, the other third were supportive straight friends. The Rainbow Union continued to meet at the College Home as this was a safe, secure and unobtrusive off-campus location for them to hang out. When he was able, Rick attended their meetings as well. Students have enough challenges trying to live away from home for the first time in their lives and being academically successful without struggling with sexual identity issues.

Black Rock State College reached its 100th birthday in 2008. What better excuse to garner some major league publicity and celebrate success? Rick and the CLT began planning the celebration in 2005. They wanted plenty of time in which to assemble stories of historical significance, to locate pictures of interest, to interview past leaders, faculty and students and to develop a book covering the college's first century. By 2007, they were well on the way toward publishing the memorial book, which would be offered for sale to alumni and other stakeholders. It would be a revenue generator and a PR tool rolled into one.

Since 2005, Bob Carlisle and Rick had been working on a Centennial Campaign to enhance the BRSC endowment by $5 million. They utilized the donor prospect research results they had obtained earlier to help construct a giving table for the campaign. They figured that to reach their goal the college needed one $1 million gift, one $500,000 gift, two $250,000 gifts, two $100,000 gifts, five $50,000 gifts and ten $25,000 gifts to total $2.7 million in the silent phase of the undertaking. Then, they thought that they could take the campaign publicly to college stakeholders to raise the remaining $2.3 million.

They decided that they needed 15 prospective donors capable of giving more than $100,000 in order to accomplish the six largest gifts. Thirty others would be needed to cover the rest of the silent phase of the campaign. They successfully identified that many from their research. Then, they prepared a case statement and went on the road beating the bushes.

It was also time to line up some centennial celebration speakers. They had selected a weekend in the late spring of 2008 to host the celebration. The speakers list included Georgia Governor Sonny Purdue, US Senators Saxby Chambliss and Johnny Isakson, Representative Nathan Deal (at this writing, Governor of Georgia), University System Chancellor Lamar Hendricks and a couple of Rick's predecessors. With a year's notice, it was fairly easy to recruit some of these leaders, most of whom were always looking for a venue in which to enhance visibility. The challenge was in second guessing who would withdraw due to more pressing issues or better exposure opportunities shortly before the event. The college needed some backup speakers to call upon on short notice, if need be. Rick, of course, would be one of these. Bill MeElhenney and Harry Rex Thornton also agreed to this arrangement.

Pulling off a quality event like this was a challenging and fun way in which to engage the entire campus in an uplifting experience for everyone.

The college needed open sided tent venues in case of rain, tons of hors d'oeuvres, barrels of punch, students to conduct campus tours, faculty to explain laboratory research, and the like. They were also able to kick-off the public phase of the Centennial Campaign in 2008, having raised close to $3 million in the silent portion of the undertaking before announcing the $5 million goal.

Chapter Thirteen

Retirement

"The heck with the pension, give me my staff!" —Rick Nedic

In the fall of 2010, the start of their 10th year at BRSC, Sally and Rick announced to the community that they would be retiring and moving to Arkansas at the end of the academic year. This allowed the college to begin a search for Rick's successor that fall so that a new leader could be in place by the time they left in the summer of 2011.

Rick had accomplished all that he thought he could at Black Rock State. Enrollment was at an all-time high thanks to the many new degree programs. The endowment was over $5 million and growing. The campus was completely wireless. Several academic buildings had undergone extensive renovation and expansion. Rick felt good about the enhancements his administration had accomplished for BRSC and its students.

He and Sally enjoyed their last year at BRSC. They were feted by student and faculty groups and had several retirement celebrations during spring semester. At commencement in May 2011, Rick surprised Sally by endowing a fund in her name to support continuing work to the benefit of a diverse student body with special emphasis on LGBT students.

After they had retired to their mountain retreat in Arkansas, Rick enrolled in a one year certificate course in motorcycle mechanics at Ozark Technical College and Sally and he began some cross-country motorcycle trips. Their son had married during their stint at BRSC and their first grandchild was born.

A college or university presidency is the very *best* job in the world! It carries with it a bully pulpit for commentary on most every aspect of society, the opportunity to make significant contributions to the lives of others, occasions to make wonderful new friends, prestige and an entrée to a great many venues otherwise unattainable. Being number two (a dean or a provost) doesn't even come close! Successful leadership is a terrific high!

While this book dwells on the challenges of Rick's experiences as a way of relating approaches to handling them, his pride in accomplishment far outshone these relatively minor bumps in the road. Rick's presidency was his self-actualization experience — he knew that he was being all that he could be. He wouldn't have missed it for anything!

Appendixes

APPENDIX I:
QUESTIONS TO ANTICIPATE FOR YOUR INTERVIEW

- What peaks your interest about this job?
- Why do you think that you are a good fit for our institution?
- What would be your highest priority activities during your first few weeks on the job?
- What are the three biggest challenges this institution will face in the next few years?
- What are your greatest strengths? Weaknesses?
- What three adjectives would others use to describe you?
- Tell us about a professional situation where you were required to implement a plan with which you were in disagreement.
- What kind of professional situations make you most uncomfortable?
- What professional accomplishment makes you most proud?
- Are you a workaholic?
- What are your professional aspirations?
- Tell us about one of your heroes.
- What do you do for recreation?
- What else would you like us to know about you?
- What questions do you have for us?

APPENDIX II:
QUESTIONS TO ASK WHEN CHECKING REFERENCES OF CANDIDATES FOR EXECUTIVE LEADERSHIP POSITIONS

Some of these derive from a CareerTrack course entitled *"How to Interview and Hire the Right People: Conducting Effective Interviews."*

- *Tell me how you know this candidate.* This provides a context to assess whether the reference is in a position to evaluate the attributes you care about. It is also a good ice-breaker.
- *Describe the position for which the person is being considered and ask if the reference thinks the candidate is capable of performing well in that capacity.* The reference may not be knowledgeable about your expectations for the candidate. This gives the reference the opportunity to react to the specifics of the circumstances.
- *How does the candidate go about developing working relationships with others?* You are trying to elicit the reference's opinion about the strength of the candidate's interpersonal skills.
- *How accepting will the candidate be to criticism designed to improve performance?* You want to assure yourself that the individual will internalize constructive feedback, learn new skills and approaches, and improve areas of weakness.
- *Does the candidate have experience evaluating the performance of others? Describe how you think he or she would handle that assignment, please.* This will, no doubt, be an important part of the new assignment for an executive team member.
- *How large a budget has this candidate been responsible for developing and managing? How would he or she deal with budget constraints?* You need to know if the potential leader can function effectively with financial responsibilities.
- *How will the candidate handle implementing unpopular decisions?* You should be aware of the extent of the candidate's courage and resourcefulness when under fire.
- *What are the candidate's greatest strengths?* This is an age old obligatory question; and, it allows you to ask about areas that the reference does not mention. It also sets up the next question.
- *What are areas in which the candidate could grow and develop?* This phrasing is better than asking for the person's *weaknesses*, since it gives the respondent the opportunity to think that they may be able to help you to enhance the person's value to your organization.
- *Tell me about your opinion of the candidate's integrity, please. What specific experiences have you had with her or him that led you to this*

conclusion?* It is critical that you evaluate the openness, honesty, forthrightness and personal integrity of candidates.
- *Would you hire the candidate for the job for which he or she is being considered?* You are trying to pin the reference down regarding their bottom line opinion of the candidate.
- *If the candidate leaves your organization, will their position be difficult to fill?* Same as the previous question.
- *What else would you like to tell me about this person?* This gives the reference an opportunity to close the conversation as he or she wishes.
- And lastly, ask *"Who else should I speak with about this person's abilities?"* Ask this of *everyone* providing information about the candidates.

APPENDIX III:
QUESTIONS TO ASK IN AN INTERVIEW OF CANDIDATES FOR POSITIONS OF EXECUTIVE LEADERSHIP

Some of these derive from a CareerTrack course entitled: *"How to Interview and Hire the Right People: Conducting Effective Interviews."*

- How would you spend your first few days on the job?
- Describe your most difficult professional assignment, please.
- What are the most applicable skills which you bring to this position? Why are these so important?
- What do you think you will enjoy most about this position? Why? Which of your skills support your opinion on this?
- What do you expect to learn from this assignment? Why is that important to you?
- For what have you been criticized in the last two years? Why did you make the decision that resulted in the criticism? What was your response to the criticism? May I discuss this issue with your current boss?
- How do you provide criticism to subordinates? What do you do, if the criticism is ignored?
- What is the professional accomplishment of which you are the most proud?
- What do you think it is that makes people successful? Why? Why do some people with appropriate credentials and ability fail?
- What motivates you? Why?
- Would you prefer to design and develop plans, or to implement them? Why?
- Tell me about the most unpopular professional decision that you ever had to implement, please. What was the result?

- What professional situations cause you to feel awkward? Why? How do you handle these?
- What are three adjectives that others would use to describe you? Why do they believe this about you?
- What is the one thing that people would say you need to improve on? Why do they feel this way about you?
- Define integrity. Describe a situation when yours has been tested.
- Describe your ideal boss.
- Describe your least ideal boss. How would you deal with a boss who has one of these least desirable attributes?
- How will you know when you have "made it" professionally?
- What are your recreational interests?
- What else would you like me to know about you?

Responses to questions like these should give you a pretty good idea of a candidate's preparation for and approach to the job, of their leadership philosophy, of their judgment, of their integrity and of their fit with you and your team.

APPENDIX IV:
PROCESS FLOW DIAGRAMS

The first step in preparing flow diagrams involves defining discrete process activities in the operation of each team or department. Start with those services delivered "where the rubber meets the road." The rubber meets the road when a service is completed and delivered to a customer. Customers may be students, parents, employers of graduates, donors, state legislators, boards of trustees, or other departments and stakeholders within the institution. A simple example of such a service is processing a payment for tuition, fees, books and supplies, room, or board.

    The institution accepts a check, credit card, or electronic payment and provides the customer with a receipt. Most customers take it for granted that money in the amount of the payment will be credited to the appropriate account. They do not give the matter any further thought. That is because most organizations have well developed processes for assuring, with a *very* high degree of accuracy, that payments are credited correctly.

    This process may vary from institution to institution; however, I can assure you that a specific sequence of steps is spelled out for employees to follow that helps to assure that the university has confidence that its actions will result in accurate transactions and customer satisfaction. None of us would put up with a service that was not near perfect at this vital activity.

Most colleges and universities have a written procedure that details actions it takes to make certain that payments end up credited to the correct account.

A flow diagram is a picture version of the list of action steps in the procedure that employees implement to accept the payment; credit the correct account; send the check or electronic payment to the issuing bank so it may deduct it from the appropriate customer account, or process the credit card payment; confirm when funds actually show up in the correct account based on the payment clearing its bank; double check for quality assurance; comply with any legal or deposit insurance requirements; and the like. In a process flow diagram, each individual step is described with a brief phrase and this phrase is placed in small box drawn on the diagram.

A brief description of the first activity in the process flow is placed at the left hand margin enclosed in its box. An arrow is drawn from this box to the right to a box containing a description of the *next* step. If there are multiple possible outcomes as a result of the first step, these are listed in separate parallel boxes, all connected back to the box to the left. Then, the next steps are listed in their respective boxes with connecting arrows always pointing to the right.

The process flow diagram progresses, box by box, across the page to the right, until the final service or outcome is delivered to the customer and completed accurately. Customers may be internal to the organization, or external to it. The diagram may require a large sheet, or even an entire wall, to complete. The last box on the right is the end of the particular function being diagrammed.

There are several commercially available software packages for creating process flow diagrams. These include smartdraw.com, accuprocess.com, edrawsoft.com, and gliffy.com.

APPENDIX V:
UNIT PRODUCTIVITY/ASSESSMENT FACTORS

Here are some assessment factors beginning with the admissions office. The college planned on receiving a projected number of applicants for enrollment for each year. The admissions office gathered applicant academic records (achievement test scores, high school transcripts, etc.), read and considered each application, and rendered an admissions decision. For borderline applications, a committee of several admissions counselors reviewed the applications together. Acceptance and rejection letters were prepared and mailed. A percentage of accepted applicants actually enrolled.

A number of unit productivity/assessment factors came to mind here. First, the effectiveness of the college's *marketing* program was accessed by determining the number of applications received per marketing dollar spent on recruitment. This factor was compared to previous years to gain insight into how it was trending.

The total number of applications considered by the Admissions Office counseling staff over a given period of time (say November through January) was easily determined. The number of applications was divided by the number of counselors reviewing the applications to calculate a unit productivity/assessment factor of the number of applications considered per counselor for the period of time in question. If we intended to increase the number of applications, this factor helped determine when we would need to add another counselor.

The same went for the clerical staff which gathered applicants' supporting materials and prepared the acceptance and rejection letters. The trend line of number of applicant files completed per staff member per week or number of acceptance/rejection letters issued per staff member per week helped determine the need for clerical position staffing.

The number of prospective student campus visits per admissions counselor per month was easily determined and useful with respect to staffing. Likewise, the dollars expended in the admissions department budget per student enrolled per year was a utilitarian parameter.

For Financial Aid Office operations, the number of student queries per counselor per year is useful, as is the dollars of aid awarded per counselor per year and the cost per aid applicant per year which may be determined by dividing the total financial aid department budget for the year by the number of applicants for aid in that year.

Unit productivity/assessment factors for library operations included the number of inquiries per work shift, the minutes of time expended per search request per library staff member, the number of library customers per day, the cost per student of providing library services (library budget divided by number of students enrolled), and the cost per library visit for providing these services (budget divided by number of library visits by students, faculty, staff, and the public).

The Registrar's Office wanted to know how many student visits it experienced each semester; the number of transfer credit requests per semester; the number of computer transactions per student per semester; and the number of individual counseling sessions per semester per registrar office employee. The Career Planning/Placement Office wished to know the number of job interviews per semester; the number of students taking interviews per semester; the cost of operations per interview (department budget divided by number of interviews); the number of offers extended per recruiting organization; and the average salary offered to graduates by degree program.

The number of student visits per Health Center professional staff member was determined, as was the budget for the Health Center on a per visit basis. The number of students per residence hall professional was useful information; as were dollars budgeted for residence hall operations per student and per dormitory building. Budget spent for Student Activities on a per student basis was worthwhile to calculate. Intercollegiate athletics budget per student-athlete was calculated on a sport-by-sport basis, so trends could be studied.

For Food Service, the cost of goods sold per student and/or per meal was useful, as well as food service staff cost per student and per meal. The number of items purchased in various cost categories per procurement professional was determined. The dollars budgeted per student for institutional safety was also informative.

Physical Plant unit productivity/assessment factors included the number of square feet of building space cleaned per day per custodian; the cost per square foot to clean buildings (budget for custodians and their supplies divided by total square footage of buildings to be cleaned daily); the number of acres of grass to be mowed per week or month per mower; the square footage of wall to be painted per employee per month; and the number of acres of gardens to be maintained per employee per month.

Factors for the Office of Institutional Advancement included the percentage of alumni contributing to the college each year; the average number of dollars contributed per participating alumnus per year; the cost of operating the office per contributing alumnus; the cost of operating the office per dollar raised; and the total gifts received (cash, stock, equipment, real property, etc.) per year.

At BRSC, they assigned every ordinary classroom (not laboratories or rooms with special functions) to the registrar for class scheduling. That assured optimum use of classroom space, as opposed to allowing academic departments to control utilization.

APPENDIX VI:
JOB DESCRIPTIONS AND PERFORMANCE EVALUATIONS

Job descriptions should be written with action verbs. For a janitorial function, the description might include: *Empties office waste baskets daily. Cleans bathroom fixtures and mops bathroom floors daily. Vacuums carpets daily.*

For a receptionist, the description may include: *Greets the public in a friendly, helpful manner. Makes arrangements for visitors to meet with organizational members. Helps visitors to feel welcome while waiting for appointments. Answers telephones politely and professionally and relays calls appropriately, and takes accurate, complete messages.*

Job descriptions for professional employees will look differently than those for support staff. A faculty member may have a position description that includes the following: *Meets classes punctually. Is well prepared for each class meeting. Posts office hours and is available to students during those hours. Contributes to attainment of departmental goals and objectives. Serves on standing institutional committees. Writes at least one successful grant proposal per year.*

An enrollment management executive's job description might contain some of the following actions. *Prepares annual enrollment targets consistent with institutional goals and objectives. Prepares budget requests in conjunction with marketing initiatives necessary to achieve enrollment targets. Identifies, hires, trains, evaluates, and rewards admissions recruiters/counselors to meet enrollment goals. Reports progress against enrollment goals at monthly meetings of the executive committee.*

Job descriptions may also detail key responsibilities regarding cooperation and coordination with other organizational entities. If the position is one of significant leadership responsibility, an organization chart may be included. Key relationships with other positions in the organization may be described. Responsibility for strategic planning for the organizational unit may be included.

Once the job description is written, annual evaluation forms should be prepared using the job description as a template. A quantitative Likert scale rating system is useful for each area of responsibility to be evaluated. For the janitorial position, the evaluation form might look as follows.

Disagree --------------Agree
(1) (2) (3) (4) (5)

Custodian

Daily Responsibilities

Empties waste receptacles.
Scrubs bathroom fixtures and mops bathroom floors.
Vacuums carpets.
Dusts furniture.
Mops uncarpeted floors.

Monthly Responsibilities

Washes windows on the inside.
Polishes uncarpeted floors with wax.
Shampoos carpets.

Personal Traits

> Is on-time for work
> Keeps running lists of equipment and supplies needed to perform job.
> Interacts with supervisor in positive and productive manner.
> Is considerate of coworkers.
> Is appropriately dressed for work every day.
> Is judicious in the use of sick leave.

The evaluation form for the receptionist might look as follows.

Receptionist

Daily Responsibilities

> Greets members of the public in a friendly manner.
> Is resourceful in referring visitors to appropriate offices for assistance.
> Takes effective telephone messages, eliciting appropriate information from caller.
> Helps visitors feel at home — offers refreshments, keeps them posted on status of appointments.
> Performs other work as assigned by supervisor.

Personal traits

> Is dressed appropriately for the position.
> Is punctual.
> Makes judicious use of sick leave.
> Is considerate of coworkers.
> Interacts effectively with supervisor.

The evaluation form for the enrollment management executive is more extensive.

Vice President of Enrollment Management

Strategic Planning

> Ably represents the division in strategic planning meetings with the Campus Leadership Team.
> Understands overall organizational goals and objectives and translates them into a coherent plan for the division
> Effectively leads members of the division in developing strategic plans in concert with overall organizational goals and objectives.
> Meets strategic goals and objectives in a timely, cost effective manner.

Enrollment

Sets achievable goals for enrollment per geographic area and by academic program.
Effectively assists admissions counselors/recruiters in achieving enrollment goals.
Develops and implements an effective marketing plan for recruiting students.
Meets annual enrollment goals.

Human Resource Management

Provides appropriate incentives for admissions office to reward them for achieving enrollment goals.
Makes timely visits to each geographic territory to review progress against enrollment goals.
Conducts annual performance reviews of direct reporting employees in the division.
Assures that every employee in the division undergoes an annual performance review with his or her supervisor.
In conjunction with the human resources department, develops an appropriate compensation package for direct reports.
Reviews compensation package for all employees in the division on an annual basis.

Budget Management

Effectively prepares divisional budgets.
Is able to manage the division within budget constraints.
Leads the departments within the division to reasonable budget requests.

Leadership

Effectively communicates organizational goals to members of the division.
Is able to identify, attract, hire, and retain an effective staff.
Creates a positive atmosphere of growth and development for direct reports.
Interacts effectively with other members of the Campus Leadership Team.
Is an effective enrollment management advisor to the CEO.

Evaluation forms should also provide space for *qualitative* feedback. This allows evaluators to write *subjective* information that may assist the person being evaluated in improving performance and/or growing personally and professionally.

www.ingramcontent.com/pod-product-compliance
Ingram Content Group UK Ltd.
Pitfield, Milton Keynes, MK11 3LW, UK
UKHW020821240326
469204UK00019B/130